WHO GOES THERE?

The Legend of Talley Bottom Ridge

By Lyn Murray

Golden Panda Publishing
USA

Dedication

To lovers of all things weird –
and to Artie for introducing me to
The Legend of Talley Bottom Ridge.

I miss you.

Who Goes There?

The Legend of Talley Bottom Ridge

Here we have a collection of short stories, facts, and discussions, about 'things that go bump in the night'. Things that we can't see – but things that are just as surely there!

Some of these things are right outside our front door, some are across the street, and some – are across the world. Sometimes they take us, sometimes they bring us back, and sometimes – *they don't!*

Some of these glitches in time even lurk in the woods of our National Parks – like Yosemite or Yellow Stone Park. In fact, many of these *vanishings* happen there – but they won't talk about it. Bad for business, I guess. But we're going to talk about it here. We're going to talk about all sorts of vanishings – before we go *poof,* too!

Just kidding! Never fear – knowledge is prevention; and if Lyn aims to do anything, it is teach and entertain us at the same time. That's how she earned her title as the "Dinner and a Movie" author; with books like these – who needs TV!

Table of Contents

Introduction

When an unsuspecting traveler stumbles into the 'wrong town' to get gas – he gets more than he bargained for, when the mysterious owner detains him from leaving by telling him that nightfall is approaching.

To get the traveler's attention, he proceeds to explain why it's important for him not to leave, and begins to tell him a story based upon a local legend, that the traveler is about to learn . . . is terrifyingly – true!

Chapter 1

Long about nightfall, with the setting sun, you won't find townsfolk milling about. 'Long about nightfall, everyone from around these parts have long since left the outdoors and gone inside to the safety of four walls behind locked doors. 'Long about nightfall. And if they hear anything outside, they don't ask – Who Goes There – not anymore. They know!

Because of what happened last night, I'm tempted to make that the starting point of this story, but unless you understand the legend you won't understand the terror that lurks in the shadows of this place – and that would be a mistake. For you. *Not for us*. We don't go out at night anymore. But you're new here, so grab a cup of coffee or whatever beverage you favor, and join me by the fire.

I guess you're not settling here, you just stopped off for gas; but I saw you looking at the lake across the road, and thought you might be thinking of walking there. Don't. It'll be getting dark soon – and there's something you should know."

A quiet stillness filled the air as the stranger dumped the last creamer into his coffee before joining me by the fire. I could tell he was a bit weary. I didn't know if it was of me – or my words. I didn't care. When you're trying to save a life, you don't stop to ask if they want to be saved – you just do it! I can take questioning looks – done it before, doing it right now. He'll get over it, and be on his way. Hopefully alive. At least, that's my goal. After he hears what I have to say – the rest is up to him. At least he's not a teen, doesn't look like a thrill seeker: mid-thirties I'd say, and from the look of his car, well healed. So, maybe he'll listen. But that remains to be seen.

The stranger pulled up a chair across from me, crossed his legs, and balanced the coffee cup on his knee. He smiled, narrowed his eyes. A curious furrow wrinkled his brow as he waited for me to speak. I guess I was dragging my feet a bit, this is hard, confiding in a perfect stranger, but it's not my first time – you'd think I'd be used to it by now. You'd be wrong.

"You had something to tell me?" The stranger asked sipping his coffee.

I nodded. "Yes. Forgive me, but this is never easy." An awkward silence followed, and I could tell he was losing patience with me, so I spoke up. "It's hard confiding in strangers, but you were looking at our lake like you were thinking of walking over while you drank your coffee – and I couldn't let you do that. Were you?"

"As a matter of fact I was. It's been a long drive, and I welcome any favorable opportunity to stretch my legs. You know how traveling is."

"I do. Although I don't travel anymore. My place is here – for folks like you. You see, my store is the only one on the Eastern outskirts of town. Passersby usually stop here first to get gas, and such, before starting up the mountain. There's another station on the other side of town for visitors coming from the West. We don't get many of those. Don't know why. It's a good thing though."

"Oh? Why is that?"

And there it was: the game of twenty-questions was over. Now I had to tell him or he'd chalk this encounter up to 'bizarro' and head out that door and drive away – without ever knowing what hit him.

I leaned forward, extended my arms, and resting my elbows on my knees – began. "Okay. Let me start at the beginning. It could take a while, but it'll make it easier."

"I'm not going anywhere. I've got all night. Take your time."

"An Englishman named William Sabre Talley, and his family settled this town back in the 1700's. Because we're located at the bottom of a ridge that separates the eastern portion of land before you hit the high mountains – he named it – Talley Bottom Ridge. As you might imagine, there's a lot written about our founding father, a lot – *but not all.*

Records indicate that Talley and his family settled here (about 195 miles South of Denver) just prior to one of the worst winters ever recorded. Whether or not Talley, and the others, were involved in a reported lost expedition and shipment of Spanish gold isn't known, but just why they settled here remains a mystery. No gold was never found. Reportedly, the Spaniards were transporting twelve chests of Spanish gold coins from Santa Fe, New Mexico to St. Augustine, Florida. The money was to be utilized for payroll and garrison expenses. The regiment, led by a man by the name of Carrasco Rodriguez, *for some reason*, traveled through Colorado rather than taking a more direct southerly route. Somewhere around where Trinidad is today, the regiment was caught in the winter weather where they were forced to stay until the spring. When spring arrived, Rodriguez reportedly led his caravan in the wrong direction, and nothing was ever heard of them again. Over the years, incoherent reports of strange happenings and disappearances have been recorded in a little known area (blocked from satellite surveillance) just south of a small mid-size, East Texas town that also bears the name – Talley Bottom. We don't know what it means – if it means anything, but I'm not predisposed to coincidences.

Interestingly enough, a wealthy ancestor of Talley's was recently found dead (an apparent suicide, authorities say) having shot himself repeatedly (over eight times) in the head and chest – with an automatic nail gun. *For no apparent reason.* Just more high-strangeness for these parts.

My guest's questioning look of doubt mirrored my own.

Anyhow, the settlers living quarters couldn't'

have been very elaborate. Obviously, they were sufficient for survival or we wouldn't be having this conversation; but by all accounts, they were sparse. A few other settlers joined them, the Ridgeways, Oremans, and the Dades from Ohio. Records show they decided to join forces to increase their chances for survival. Which they did.

It's not clear if they built one shelter or several, but logic has them building one shelter large enough to accommodate everyone until the spring thaw. One thing you have to understand, these people were pioneers. They were use to hardships that would kill us today. Not a tenderfoot among them. Even the kids, the combined total about eight, the oldest being fourteen, were wilderness wise. *Seasoned survivors.* Like most Pioneers.

Anyway, some time after the shelter was built and the families had moved out of their wagons and into it – things began to get really strange. Food stored outside started turning up missing. Items from the wagons started vanishing, that sort of thing. They dismissed most of it as animal related. The missing stuff from the wagons was a little harder to explain. Indians were thought to be behind it.

But as the winter progressed, and because so much of their things had been taken, and ransacked through, the men decided to hold nightly vigils outside. They'd build a fire and take two-hour shifts guarding the area. According to documents, that's when the strangeness ramped up.

An entry from one of the Ridgeway girl's diary explains that an hour into the first night's vigil, by her father, Timothy Ridgeway, they heard a loud scream, and of course, everyone ran outside to see what had happened. And that's when they saw Ridgeway's lantern laying on its side at the edge of the house. But no Ridgeway. First, they thought wolves, or bears, but there was no blood. He was just gone. Without a trace.

The rest of the men took up watch together and spent the night outside. By early morning, everyone was dressed and out searching the area for signs of Ridgeway. They never found him. However, stranger still – there were no footprints leading to beside the house where the lantern was found – except theirs, and none leading behind the house and into the woods. *None.*

The next night, two men – not one, set up vigil

outside. Nothing happened. The night was quiet. Eerily quiet, to read Ridgeway's daughter's next entry into her diary. But the next morning they would find that it had not been as quiet as they thought, well, quiet maybe, but they hadn't been alone.

Around back, as the women were fetching water from the hot-spring near the lake – embedded deep in the snow, they found huge footprints that could not have come from any known source – human or animal. Just a string of large, rumor has them some thirty inches in length, indefinable three toed, large clawed footprints, (but definitely footprints of something) that ended as suddenly as they began. They just stopped in the middle of nowhere. They began in the middle of nowhere – they stopped in the middle of nowhere. And something else – Ridgeway's glove. His left glove was found near the footprints. Just his left, and nothing more."

My guest asked, "What?! And blood?"

"Nope! Not a drop!"

"That's impossible! Isn't it? He went somewhere. Something happened to him, and I doubt that he went willingly. There had to have been signs of a struggle."

"You'd think so. But, no. Nothing. But it gets weirder."

"I'm all ears." He said getting up to refresh his coffee. "Continue, please."

I remember the sun was setting, the last remains of the day shone through the glass at the front of the store, casting strange shadows on the old, hardwood floor from the marquee outside. When my guest returned to the fire, his gait was more energetic than before. This time he quickly took his seat, easily settling into the rickety, old, captains chair he had so stiffly occupied earlier. Stories have that effect on people – at least all those who have occupied the chair before me – under similar circumstances. And, yes, there have been more than a few. But, I digress, so I'll continue.

"The next few nights were quiet, no thefts, no noise and no disappearances – and then..."

"Don't tell me someone else disappeared?"

"Not someone; some thing."

"What do you mean? Some thing? A thing?"

"The Dade's wagon."

"What, a whole wagon? Gone?!"

"Yep! Just gone."

"You mean drove away, right?

"Nope."

"What are you saying?!"

This is usually where my guest stands up. This one did not surprise me.

Standing up and walking to warm himself by the fire – like all those before him – he turned with astonishment, and disbelief chiseled upon his face, with the usual accompanying words [B.S. or Bull Hockey for the faint-hearted], but struggling to suppress them under his breath, as deep furrows drew tight against his forehead. Then he spoke.

"You're telling me a whole wagon just vanished? Just like that? Just gone? No trace? And you expect me to believe it? He sharply paused. Rural prank, right, played on unsuspecting passersby, right? Like the five-leg Turkey, my Grandpa use to tell us kids about. You held me here for this? Come on!"

This is where I nod my head up and down, like one of those silly dash-dogs, and say something reassuring like, "Yes, it's not a prank." They always look at me the same way: mouth open, lip curled to one side, with a queer look on their face. You know the one. Before continuing, I urge them to come back and take a seat. The last thing I need is someone bouncing off the walls, because like all the nights past, this one has just begun – and of the two people in this room, I alone know what's coming; and I've got to keep him here – 'till dawn.

"Sit, please." I said, with a motioning gesture.

This is where my guest reluctantly returns to their seat. That look still plastered across their face, as if it had been stamped there. One of unadulterated fear would soon replace it. But there was nothing I could do about that. I didn't ask him to stop here. Wish he hadn't. But that's like closing the gate after the horse has fled the corral, and does just about as much good. He's here. Another poor unsuspecting soul who thinks they've got a

handle on things – when they don't know jack!
He's about to get a lot smarter!

Chapter 2

This is where I ask, "You okay? You want me to continue?" To which they always reply, "What, stop now? No way! Continue."

"Back to the wagon. Yes, it was just gone. No tracks, just like with Ridgeway – no tracks. Just like it was picked up, straight up, and taken away. The odd thing was ..."

"Odder than that? That's gonna take some do'en – pal!"

"Yeah, if you can believe it – odder than that."

I guess I paused a little too long, because my guest blurted out, "Well?"

"Sorry, I've told this story hundred's of times, and it never gets old. Let me continue. Odd thing was, beside the wagon tracks, where it had been sitting, was a strange metallic object. It's at the museum in town. You can see it tomorrow if you're still here. Opens at 9."

[The look on his face told me that he had taken the bait. It always worked. Hooks 'em every time. He'd be safe now. Tomorrow he'd be on his way, after a quick stop by the museum; then me, and this town, would fade into history along with his other memories, becoming nothing more than a sleepless, late night story. *Or not.*]

Just then, the lights went out. And like all the

times before, my newest guest rose to his feet with a start.

"It's nothing." I urged him to sit back down. I hadn't lied; it was nothing, *not yet.*

"What's go'en on?"

"I told you. Strange things happen around here at night. That's all. You'll be safe enough inside. They never come inside."

"They? Who they? What never comes inside?"

"Them. We don't know who or what they are. Never seen them. They stay well out of sight. We just hear them. Find things gone, landscape disturbed, that sort of thing. We haven't had any disappearances in over ten years. Well, until last night, that is. But I couldn't tell him anything. He stopped off for gas, just like you – but he wasn't interested in hearing about the legend. *I tried.* I just couldn't stop him."

"Couldn't stop him from what? Speak up man – you're scaring me!"

"Couldn't stop him from leaving before daylight."

"And....?   And....? What, he's gone? Disappeared? Will you speak up, spit it out?!"

"Yes. Gone. That's his car at the curb. No keys to move it, he was carrying them when it happened."

"When what happened!? Good god, will you get to it – the suspense is killing me!"

"It was just about this time, just after dusk, after the sun set behind the trees. I begged him not to go outside, but he thought I was just another crazy, old loon whose been living alone too long. I tried to hold him back, but he broke free of my grip, and rushed out. I couldn't follow him. You understand – I couldn't follow him. I couldn't!"

"Yes, yes, I understand. Please, what the hell happened? What did you see?"

"Nothing. Nothing at all. Nothing except that strange, swirling light that always precedes a disappearance."

"What light? What in heaven's name are you babbling about?"

"That's what I'm trying to tell you. It only

happens at night. Just at night. And not every night. Sometimes we go months without anything missing. Then, boom, right out of the blue – it comes back. Takes things. Animals. People if they're outside. That's why we don't go outside after dark. You see, don't you? You see why I couldn't let you leave?"

"I don't know what I see. I know you're scared of something. Of what, I don't know. I hear the words you're saying, but I'm having a hard time applying them to anything I'm familiar with."

He paused. *They always do.*

"Let me get this straight."

He sipped his coffee, which had to be cold by now, but he drank it down as if it was the best coffee he'd ever had.

"Let me get this straight. You people, the people living in this town, are being stalked by something you've never seen, something that's been around since the late 1700's, something that periodically comes in, or with some sort of light, and takes things? People and things. Is that right?"

"Yes."

"Are you telling me that you're being visited by Aliens? Space Aliens? Or possibly, some kind of alien creature from another dimension? Because that's what it sounds like you're saying. Is that what you're saying?"

"I never said Aliens."

"No, but you're alluding to it (or something even stranger), and I'm giving it a name I can relate to. Well, not that I can really relate, but I'm more comfortable (if that's possible) calling it – they, them, Aliens. At least it's a word I'm familiar with."

I urged him, "Sit down. There's more."

He took his seat, and shaking his head from side to side, said, "I'll be honest with you, I don't know if I can take much more; but I'm here – I'm not about to leave, so, go ahead. Shoot. I guess!"

"Whenever the light comes and the disappearances start – there is a slight humming sound. But it doesn't come from the sky. When you think of Aliens, you think sky. This comes from the ground. That's why we don't call our – visitors – Aliens. And the strange, swirling light doesn't seem to come from the sky either. It just appears. And then it's gone."

"Like a vortex? You're describing a vortex."

"I don't know. I guess. That's as good a name as any."

"Okay, you said the guy last night walked back outside, through your door – that door [he said pointing toward the front] and immediately vanished? Immediately?"

"Pretty much. He got about halfway to his car, and poof!"

"You saw it?"

"I saw it."

"But you can't describe it? You can't tell me what you saw, can't be more descriptive?"

"No. And you won't find anyone in this town who can."

"Unbelievable! And you people just sit here and take it. You don't call authorities. Why?"

"Because they disappear, too. You see, they don't believe us. They always have to test the water. Venture out. And then it's too late! Finally, we just stopped calling."

"But surely, if what you're telling me is true, someone comes looking for them. I mean, people don't just vanish into thin air, not without someone taking notice. Do they?

"Here they do. Oh, authorities take notice all right, but ..."

"Then why don't they shut this place down? Close the roads. Something?"

"Because they can't."

"What do you mean they can't?"

"It's the final piece to this unsolvable puzzle."
"What is?"

"The land grants. It's in the land grants. It goes back to the 1800's; when the United States was formed the government claimed this area "off limits" as far as local and state jurisdiction is concerned."

"Off limits – what does that mean? Off

limits?"

The lights flickered again; static electricity filled the air with a whooshing sound. Always does.

This is where I usually need to change the course of the conversation. You'll understand why in a minute, so bear with me.

My guest jumped. "What is that?"

"I wish I could say, but I can't. Don't know. It just happens."

"Is it them?

"Probably. But you'll be safe enough as long as ..."

"As long as I stay inside. Right? Count on it. But, what keeps them from coming inside? That's just got to be the craziest thing I ever heard. Oh, sure, take 'em outside – just don't come inside. Dan Aykroyd was right! Cow lips – take all you want. Nuts! That's what that is, nuts!"

"I agree, but it's part of the agreement."

"Ah, yes, the agreement with the government. About that . . . "

"Wait." *I have to interrupt them here to explain the dynamics of the agreement, or they go off on a mind-blowing tangent from which there is no return, so I quickly ask,* "How did you find this place? How did you end up here? GPS? . . . Map?"

This is always where they say, "No. Just came down the river road, through that pass, and there you were. Don't remember seeing you on the map. GPS was no help. I was almost out of gas – and suddenly there you were."

He paused. *They always do.*

"Hey. Why aren't you on the map?"

This is where I remind them that I'm trying to explain. "If you'll sit back down and let me finish. Please." *If I had to say please one more time, well, let's just say that my not so gentle side would rear its ugly head.* "Please – [damn] take your seat, and allow me to finish."

My guest looked flustered, *I could relate,* but he was more inquisitive than most, and I found it hard to control the conversation. Oh, not because I feared him venturing outside (by now, he was acutely aware of that danger) – because he was trying to run things, and I couldn't let that happen, he had to understand. I could tell by the way he kept interrupting me – that it was going to be a long night. Then a fleeting thought came to mind: maybe I should, you know, let him go outside? But, no. I couldn't do that to my worst enemy – well, maybe my worst enemy, which my guest was quickly approaching the rank of – *but no.*

"Mr. . . . ." I paused, realizing that I didn't know my guests' name. "I'm sorry, but I forgot to introduce myself." I extended my hand. "Maxwell. Maxwell Oreman. Pleased to meet you, Mr. . . . ?"

"Jennings. Bret Jennings," he said, extending his. "Just Bret."

"Well, Bret, it's my pleasure. As I was saying, and as you mentioned, you didn't find us, didn't find Talley Bottom Ridge on your map – because it's not there. Not on any map. *Ever.* Won't be. Part of the agreement with the government. Stated clearly in our town charter. By the way, we're a no fly zone, as well."

"No kidding?"

"No kidding."

"That tells me that the government knows something – they're not telling you. But what? And Why?"

He paused. *They always pause here.*

"I've got a question – why do you all stay here? I don't understand? Why don't you leave this place?"

"Can't. Know too much. [There was more truth than fiction in that statement.] They, the government won't let us, or should I say – they *strongly* prefer us not leaving. They so strongly prefer it that we are subsidized to stay. Quite handsomely, I might add. We are, for all intent and purposes, land locked. A few people like yourself wander in and out, from time to time, but as you no doubt noticed driving in – we're pretty isolated. However, to answer your question honestly – we wouldn't leave if we could. We protect this place, or rather – we protect travelers (like yourself) who happen through. It's not a glorious job –

pay sucks." (I had to laugh.) "Actually, there is no pay – we just live tax free. Mostly, we stay out of a sense of obligation. Sometimes, it's a heavy burden."

"No pay? Tax free? Income tax free?! I call that quite an incentive. I can imagine it would be burdensome, though. What about me? What obligation am I under?

"Only to survive the night – and be on your way. We do ask that you not disclose our whereabouts. Oh, sure, we realize you're going to tell the story, but please, for the safety of others (and yourself, because the government knows you're here – never doubt it) – don't divulge our whereabouts. That's our only request. Job's hard enough without a bunch of thrill seeking lunatics running around getting snatched."

Now *he* laughed.

"Damn, lifelong scrutiny – 'Men in Black', huh?; but I understand. Sort of makes me part of this now, doesn't it? Makes me a guardian, too – or *prisoner*. I would like to know what the hell I'm guarding people from, but . . ." *He looked toward the front, toward outside.* "I'm not go'en out there to find out. If what you say is true, it's a one-way trip I'm not willing to make!"

"Indeed. Wise choice!"

The lights flickered again. This time my guest didn't flinch, didn't even get up out of his chair, but merely looked at me, and said, "I might make a detour to Texas; now – tell me about that wagon."

And I did.

We talked 'till dawn.

Secret Vanishings

Our National Parks

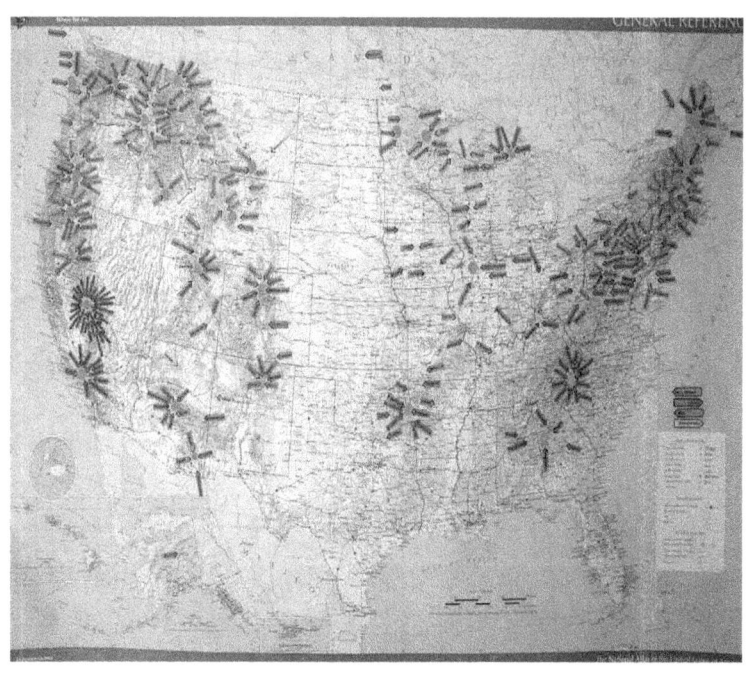

44

Strange Similarities Between Disappearances

Most of those who have disappeared are children ages 20 months to 12 years, and the elderly between 74 to 85. Not one person carrying a firearm, and only one carrying a transponder – (a transponder is an electronic device used to wirelessly receive and transmit electrical signals) like a transponder radio.

Typically, a search is initiated, and runs for about ten days before it's dropped. Fifty percent of the children who go missing are found dead, and the ones who are found, are found miles away from where they disappeared, in areas seemingly impossible for them to get to on their own.

Yosemite National Park (with 40 to 45 cases) has the largest cluster of vanishings, and oddly, in most areas where the disappearances have occurred, *huckleberries* are usually in great abundance. This raises questions, like: 1) are the abductors trying to put their abductee back into areas where they can find sustenance until they're found by search parties? or 2) in the case of small children, do these abductors not understand that children (especially very small children) don't understand that these berries are food that

45

will keep them alive until they're found (keeping in mind that small children may not even realize someone is looking for them), or – and most disturbing 3) that the abductors are just toying with their captives, and don't care whether they live or die, but just want to see what happens when they abandon them in the wilderness? Because if they cared, rational thinking dictates that they would return their captives to the original location of the abduction, making rescue a certainty. Makes you wonder, doesn't it?

Many of the areas that people have disappeared from carry such names as Devil's Gulch, Devil's Lookout, Twin Devil Lake, and Devil's Punch Bowl. Perhaps named to reflect the evil that people have sensed in these places over time? Makes you wonder, doesn't it?

The majority of children who have disappeared had dogs with them. In some cases, the dogs returned, but the children never did. In 95 percent of the cases, bad weather strangely follows a disappearance, washing out footprints and other clues and making it impossible to carry on a search until the weather clears.

In 98 to 99 percent of the cases, tracking dogs

are unable to find a scent or simply refuse to track. Now, that's just odd – they refuse to track? Maybe it's because they know (or sense) something we're too stupid to pick up.

Almost 98 percent of the disappearances occur in the afternoon. Another peculiarity that, perhaps, we should pay closer attention to.

Searchers have been known to cover an area over 100 times, only to later find the person, (alive or dead) in the same area that had earlier been searched. Children found alive won't talk about their experience, or just say they don't remember what happened to them. They're found usually running a low-grade fever and appear traumatized. In all cases, the parents say that the child was right behind them when they disappeared.

Usually, the children are wearing bright, colorful clothing when they disappear, and even if they are found miles away without the shoes they were wearing, their feet are not scratched or bruised.

Bright colors? I've heard that warning before – don't wear bright clothing in the woods; which goes against everything we're taught. We wear bright clothing to keep some gun-happy idiot from mistaking us for a deer or something. Now we're being told NOT to wear bright clothes.

Maybe we should restrict our use of bright colors to National Parks. Sounds like a good idea; but I'm not going in the woods at home without something that differentiates me from game. *Too many shooters in my state!*

◇◇◇

Ah, yes, bright colors – the warning comes from Indonesia.

Many people are disappearing in the jungles of Indonesia, apparently due to a very unusual form of abduction that takes place if they wear certain colors. *Bright clothes.* Some are returned, but generally with no memory of what happened to them.

The people of Indonesia say that ***Jin Kurcaci*** are taking people. ***Jin Kurcaci*** means little demon people. These things do what is called "penculikan" or abduction.

No one knows why they do this; but sometimes the people come back after a bit. The people or creatures have small noses, and small, black eyes, but their mouths are very broad, and when they smile, it is disproportionately large when compared to the rest of their face.

Abductees cannot remember the color of their abductor's skin, and frequently, even though they are abducted from a crowd of people – no one else can see them but the person being abducted, even though their companions are looking right at them.

▼

Some Strange Missing Person Cases

One of the first documented cases was that of Ape Canyon back in 1924 – fully discussed in my other book, *The Tuck*.

◇◇◇

Then in 1938 –

In the Rocky Mountain National Park in 1938, a husband and wife hiked high into the park and sat down to rest. Looking up high above them on a cliff in an area called The Devil's Nest, they spotted a small boy all alone. Thinking the foolish parents were nearby, the couple moved on and later drove home.

As they arrived in the valley below, they saw as many as 2500 people mulling about, but didn't stop to ask what was going on. The next morning they saw a photo of the missing child in the newspaper, and recognizing him as the child they had seen, they drove back to the park to tell the searchers, but the young boy was never found.

Again in 1952 –

A 2-year-old boy was visiting his grandparents in Ritter, Oregon, when he disappeared. He was found unconscious 19 hours later in a frozen creek bed. To arrive there (in 19 hours) the small toddler would have had to run non-stop 12 miles across two mountain peaks. Quite impossible considering his age and size.

In 1981 –

Young girls also disappear in the national parks. In Yosemite in 1981, a 14 year-old girl was backpacking on horseback with her parents, and a group of people, up 9200 feet to Sunrise High Sierra Camp. When they stopped to rest, the girl asked if she could venture away with another backpacker (a 70 year-old man) – some 50 feet away to take photos.

After reaching their destination, the old man sat down on a log, while the girl went to the edge of an elevation to get a shot of a lake down below. To get a better look, and better shot, she reportedly walked down the hill – and never came back.

More recently –

In another Yosemite case, a young woman was found dead at the bottom of a high cliff from where it seemed she had been thrown. It was determined that she had been assaulted "after" her fatal fall.

1971 –

In a few cases, Green Berets have surprisingly shown up to join and/or take over searches. This happened in 1971 in Newcomb, New York when an 8 year-old boy vanished while walking back to a lodge to change his clothes. His scent was lost in a swamp and he was never found.

2014 –

The latest disappearance is of a 34-year-old California firefighter who vanished with his dog on Friday, June 13, 2014 in the Los Padres National Forest in California. He was camping with a friend when he (reportedly) ran off shoeless, chasing his dog downhill toward a stream. I ask you, who goes off shoeless in these surroundings – unless mesmerized into forgetting all safety? But, you may ask, mesmerized by what? I don't know – but something caused this firefighter to throw 'caution to the wind'.

Another curious thing, why did his dog just take off and not come back when he called after him?

This whole account is just too weird for words.

The man's friends searched for hours, then had to hike two days out of the wilderness to find help. The area being searched is two times the size of the Grand Canyon. On June 19, the firefighter's dog was found alive.

Then on June 6, 2014

Mike Herdman, the California firefighter who disappeared two weeks earlier while chasing his dog during a backpacking trip to the Los Padres National Forest – was found dead June 27.

Like others who have disappeared into the national forests, Herdman was found at approximately 1200 feet above the river bottom, which he had chased his dog into the day he disappeared. When his remains were discovered, authorities were astonished to find him shoeless. Of course, we all know that he ran off shoeless – the astonishing thing to me is – *WHY?*

This man was a seasoned firefighter – he knew his way around, what to do, and how to act, and now he's gone! All we are left with is the knowledge that rescue crews spent nearly 5,000 man-hours searching, covering 50 square miles on foot to find the object of their search dead.

The question remains, was he beguiled into his actions – by something that lured the dog away? We'll never know – but I'm not going anywhere near a national park! I've lived this long without visiting one.

Arizona Twilight Zone

Mysterious Mountains

(Excerpts from the life of *Ron Quinn*)

Adventurer Extraordinaire

A real-life Twilight Zone may exist in Southeastern Arizona near the Mexican border.

The Treasure Hunters, from left to right:
Ron Quinn, Chuck Quinn,
Roy Purdie and Walter Fisher.
(1930's)

◇◇◇

Set deep within the mountains, close to the Mexican border, a mysterious place exists where time is randomly altered.

What?! A joke? Not according to Ron Quinn.

Quinn first submitted his stories to *The Weekly's* former editor, Michael Parnell, in November 2002. Upon his departure the following January, Parnell passed them to his successor, Jimmy Boegle.

That's when The Weekly staff decided to publish them; after all, they are quite compelling. Plus, Quinn has some credibility: as a life-long treasure hunter, his stories have appeared in *Arizona Highways, Treasure Magazine* and *Fate.* So, it wasn't much of a stretch for *The Weekly.*

However, Quinn never told The Weekly (or anyone else) the exact location of the site – so his comments were never verified; and, therefore, can only be presented as interesting stories, and nothing more.

I prefer to see his unwillingness to reveal the site's location, as one of protecting the innocent – but believe what you will.

This fascinating journey into the unknown began one unsuspecting day in early 1956, and to this day, it remains unsolved, and tantalizes all who hear it.

Like many exciting gambles, it all began during a two-year adventure into Southern Arizona in search of lost mines and hidden Spanish treasures. High among the rugged terrain bordering Mexico, Quinn and his brother Chuck discovered a location where time itself is altered. He reports that this natural freak of nature lies deep within a region – seldom visited by modern man.

He states that his reason for bringing this tale to light (after all this time) is because something 'progress related' might affect this interesting place. The Tucson Electric Power Company plans on building a 345,000-watt high-voltage transmission line from Tucson to Nogales, and the line could come quite close to the site.

Quinn's afraid that when this line becomes active, what (if anything) will this enormous voltage do to this delicate location: will it enhance the natural flow of energy that's already lurking within it (possibly sending things spiraling out of control, causing untold chaos) or do nothing at all? Only time will tell.

In any case, the following stories all took place around this mysterious, unknown location.

Unexplained Lights

Quinn states that this all began after his discharge from the military. "My brother Chuck asked if I'd be interested in taking an lengthy trip to Arizona to search for numerous legendary lost treasures purportedly hidden during the Spanish occupation. This ignited my adventurous spirit, so plans were made. We saved enough money, with the help of our parents, for two years. I was 23, and Chuck was 26.

We departed Tacoma, Wash., on March 20, 1956. Our final target was Arivaca, Ariz., a small desert colony of perhaps 70 residents. This old adobe village was located squarely in the center of the country harboring some of these well-known hidden treasures.

About three weeks into this treasure hunt, Chuck and I were relaxing at camp one evening. Towards the south, the craggy peaks of the Tumacacori Mountains were silhouetted against the darkening sky.

Suddenly, our attention was directed toward two large balls of blue-green lights slowly descending behind the mountains that were several miles away. They were not flares, as no sound of aircraft broke the stillness of the night. Within minutes, both had vanished from sight.

The following night at exactly the same time, 8:05 p.m., the lights appeared once again, near the same location. These also disappeared behind the peaks.

Several days later, Louie Romero, a local cowboy who rode for the Arivaca Ranch, stopped by. Over several weeks, we became friends and learned a great deal from him about the history of the area. While in Arivaca, we heard from the residents that if Louie conveys something, you can bet your life it's fact.

During one of his weekly stopovers, Louie told us numerous stories centering around the nearby mountains. Some bordered on the paranormal. After describing the odd lights we had seen, he smiled, saying he and others have spotted them many times since 1939 in the same location. Over the months, we saw them several more times."

Gateway to the Gods

"One day, as we were returning to Arivaca, we spotted an old truck parked beside the road with a flat tire. Not having a spare, the gentleman stood beside his vehicle trying to hitch a ride to the nearest service station. We picked him up and soon arrived at the Kinsley Ranch, and gas station.

After having the tire fixed, we returned John, an Indian, to his truck where we mounted the tire for him. John couldn't thank us enough, as not many white men had shown him such compassion.

A month or so later at camp, we spotted a rider approaching, and were surprised to see that it was John. Hc told us hc was working temporarily for a local ranch, checking the fence lines.

While speaking in general about the nearby country, Chuck mentioned we were treasure hunting. As a boy, John said he heard many of the tales of lost mission gold and silver. He also understood some of the tales were true, as treasure was found in 1907 near Nogales.

Later, John told us about a mysterious stone archway. Roy told him we came across such a formation south of camp. John's first words were, "Did you walk through its opening?"

Walt answered, "No. We noticed it while descending a slope, but paid little attention to the oddity."

John told us around the 1800s, three Indians were hunting, and upon returning to their village, discovered a stone archway. Being in a jubilant mood, they began horsing around, chasing one another through the opening.

Moments later, one of them jumped through but never appeared from the opposite side. Fearing they had entered some sacred ground of the gods, the remaining two fled the scene. Arriving at the village, they told the medicine man how their friend had disappeared before their eyes.

As the story spread, others journeyed to the high plateau to gaze upon the stone structure. Rocks and other items were tossed through, but nothing occurred, until an elderly woman approached. Tossing in a live rabbit, it suddenly vanished. The Indians backed off in fear and spread the story of this "Doorway to the Gods," as it came to be known.

John himself has been to the site on many

occasions. The only time he witnessed anything strange was around 1948. A big storm had blown in, and the sky was filled with dark clouds in all directions. As he rode past the archway, he noticed the sky through its opening was blue--no clouds were visible. Dismounting, he walked cautiously toward the formation and peered through. The mountains on the other side hadn't changed, but the sky was clear. Looking around the corner of the structure, the sky was once again covered with dark clouds. Fear gripped him and he rode off.

Some believe John was looking into another time period through the portal. We asked John: If the story was indeed true, why hadn't it been investigated? He replied that only his people knew of the story, as it had never been mentioned outside the tribe. The only reason he told us was because we had shown him kindness while stranded beside the highway.

Curious, we decided to make another trip to the remote site with Roy Purdie and Walter Fisher, two fellow treasure hunters who were camping with us. It's a rugged climb, and the torturous, craggy mountains play no favorites. Enter their domain, make an error, and you'll be added to the list of the injured and missing.

This mysterious area is covered with

windswept rock formations that dot the landscape. Searching further, we discovered an enormous deposit of geodes. The ground was littered with them. Some had broken open, revealing their crystal-lined interiors.

As we approached the archway, the structure took on a menacing appearance. It stood beside a rocky slope, and was perhaps 7 feet high by 5 feet in width. Its columns measured approximately 15 inches in diameter and were made of andesite.

Chuck jokingly tossed several rocks through, but nothing happened. Next, I placed my arm in. Roy, the superstitious member of our foursome, said I was flirting with danger if the story was true. Knowing his nature towards the unknown, I decided to play a joke. I suddenly yelled, like something was pulling me through. Jumping back, I began laughing as Roy cussed me out. By now, we were all close friends, so no offense was taken.

After several hours we departed this interesting location, carrying a number of geodes. I remember glancing back at this lonely part of the world, wondering if there was truly something within the area that could alter time at random. Was it just the archway itself, or were other unknown natural forces at play?"

They were (unfortunately) destined to discover the answer, at least to the time-altering question.

Phantom Horses

"It was roundup time on the Arivaca Ranch. That evening, Louie and several others were camping beside the corral just north of the mountains to get an early start the following morning.

As they sat around having coffee and making small talk, Louie noticed how still the night was. Most evenings, one could hear the night sounds of the desert. But this time it was unusually quiet, and the livestock seemed restless.

As they were about to bed down, they suddenly heard the rumbling of approaching horses. As the sound grew closer, one could hear the clattering of hoofs among the rocks accompanied by the whinnying of many horses. As the sound increased, the boys dove for cover, expecting to see a herd of horses stampeding through camp. But as the rumbling reached the opposite side of a nearby canyon, it abruptly ended.

The following morning, they searched, but found no evidence of horses. Louie mentioned wild horses once roamed the country around the turn of the century. Were Louie and the others caught on the outer edge of some time change?

It turns out they were near our mysterious archway.

(Before continuing, I'd like to set forth a theory told to us by a party well-versed in the field of the strange and paranormal: perhaps an enormous deposit of geodes beneath the surface might be effecting time in some mysterious manner. When all the natural elements --the vibration of the crystals, the electricity in the atmosphere and the magnetic fields in the earth--come together at the precise moment, laws of nature are turned topsy-turvy, and things occur beyond our understanding. It could be like dropping a stone into a pool of calm water--the archway being the stone and the waves expanding outward could be the natural forces. These might reach anywhere from several yards to a mile. Depending upon the activation, everything within this radiating circle could be thrown into a different period of time. When it fades, things return to normal.")

Ghostly Priest

This story was told by a reliable rancher and also took place within the shadows of the puzzling archway. It involves the appearance of a Spanish padre long since dead: a ghost, or perhaps not.

Several hundred years earlier, a Jesuit priest, whose name has long since been forgotten, built a small mission east of Arivaca. The residents gave their most treasured possessions to him for safe-keeping, as they feared robbery. These were hidden somewhere near the church grounds.

One morning, a Mexican woodchopper found the elderly padre dead. After he was put to rest, the villagers suddenly realized that he was the only one who knew the location of their valuables. They searched, and searched, but nothing was ever found.

Over the years, many cowboys and others have reported seeing a dark-robed figure walking near the site of the old mission, which has long since crumbled back into the dry earth. The description given resembles that of a Spanish padre. One rancher told us quite frankly, "Nobody will ever convince me otherwise. I know what I saw that afternoon.

The figure wasn't any ghost. It walked across a wash disturbing the gravel and casting a long shadow."

Reportedly, the figure slowly became transparent, shimmered several times then vanished.

Again, was the witness caught in another trick of time produced by the site? Or was he himself back in the 18th century, watching the padre going about his daily rounds? Too bad our rancher didn't see the mission. That would be hard evidence that he had traveled back in time.

Phantom Soldiers

Another mind-boggling story involves two cowboys out searching for a sick bull. Both separated and rode off in different directions. One rider paused atop a hill while searching the countryside below with his binoculars. Suddenly, he felt a stone bounce off his hat. Turning, he expected to find his companion had jokingly tossed it, but nobody was there. Another stone hit his arm, but once again nothing was seen.

While scanning the terrain again, he spotted his friend several hundred yards below. In the distance, he saw the bull. Waving, he shouted to his partner signaling to him which direction to go.

While descending the hill, he spotted a group of six riders traveling eastward. They rode in single file and were about half a mile away.

Stopping, he looked through his field glasses-- and was amazed at what he saw. His description of the horsemen resembled pictures he had seen of Spanish soldiers with tunics, lances and helmets. He followed their movements until the scene "shimmered" and faded.

Once again, this occurred near the archway's domain. A column of soldiers traveling east?! The only fort in that direction was the old, located at Tubac during the Spanish occupation – a couple hundred years ago.

The Presidio has served as a military reservation from its establishment in 1776 as Spain's northern-most outpost of colonial power in the New World. It was one of the longest-garrisoned posts in the country and the oldest installation in the American West. It played a key role in Spain's exploration and settlement of the borderlands, Mexico's subsequent control of the region from Texas to Alta California, and the United States' involvement not only in frontier expansion, but also in all major conflicts since the Mexican-American War of 1846-48.

◇◇◇

Skeletal Remains

Then, during the mid-1940s, Louie and another ranch hand came upon the skeletal remains of (what appeared to be that of) an ancient Indian. Beside the body was a rotted bow. The Indian's clothing was of animal skins, and a leather moccasin clung to one foot. The skull and one leg were missing.

Could this have been the Indian who vanished so long ago? The body was discovered less than a mile south of our strange location.

They buried the remains nearby, marking the grave with several large rocks. Louie noted that the body didn't resemble 200-year-old remains."

How odd!

Before hearing the above tale, Quinn said that he often wondered what became of the Indian that was allegedly swallowed by the archway. Stating, "If the portal was visible from the opposite side, why didn't he come back through? He might have never noticed a change and, to him, his friends had disappeared. Not finding them, he eventually returned to his village and perhaps also found it missing. Perhaps he was somehow transported forward in time, and for some unknown reason, died on that lonely hillside, only to be found by Louie years later."

Strange Shimmer

One day, Quinn said that Walt and Roy had their own weird experience near the stone portal. They returned there because Walt wanted to collect some geodes for friends in Tucson.

Looking toward the archway, both saw it appear to shimmer. According to Walt, this lasted several minutes before it slowly faded. During this period, both felt a strange pressure within their ears.

Roy said, "That's it Walt. I'm outta here." After gathering a number of geodes, both left, with Roy hastily leading the way.

During summer months, desert temperatures can reach 110 degrees. The heat waves dancing off a flat surface can make objects appear to shimmer while looking through them. This anomaly is called a mirage. But this was mid-January and the temperature was around 60 or so.

Mirage or something else – Old Roy would never again return to the site, no matter how we tried to persuade him.

Was the shimmering and ear sensation the beginning of some activation that never reached its full potential? Seeing the expression on Roy's face after he returned to camp, take my word, it happened."

Ghostly Camp

Over the years, a number of individuals have disappeared from the unfriendly, rugged hills. Did some make the unfortunate mistake of entering the portal at the wrong time? The following certainly suggests that possibility.

Quinn states: "While the four of us were checking out an old silver workings, we came upon a deserted miners camp that Louie had told us about weeks earlier. Everything was left behind--rotted clothing, tools, drill steel, old blankets and cooking utensils. Everything was there to maintain a functional camp. By appearances, the site was active during the 1930s.

It looked as though somebody just walked away and never returned--or couldn't. The camp was almost a mile from the bizarre site high above. Did this party fall victim to it, or did he become discouraged with mining, and abandon camp? I find this highly unlikely.

We also heard a story about a lone prospector who arrived each October and remained until spring. This continued for several years. One day, he vanished, leaving his horse, wagon and camp behind. It was located near a saddle in the mountains – just north of you know what – you know where! *A body was never found.*

We visited this site and found a deep shaft nearby with numerous open cuts on a hill. So, was he prospecting or treasure hunting? It was rumored that some bandit's loot (two bags of gold coins) was buried within this area.

It's stories like this keep people like us searching; and folks like you – reading."

Heavenly Stones

"Another close encounter occurred about 14 months into our treasure hunt, a hunt that seemed to be going nowhere.

While in Arivaca picking up needed supplies, we met three other treasure seekers. They were in the area for a month seeking the famous "Lost Treasure of Carreta Canyon" hidden by the fleeing padres from the Tumacacori Mission during the great Pima uprising of 1751.

We invited them to stop by camp, and gave them directions. Several weeks later, they arrived and had an interesting story of their own to tell.

By chance, while traveling overland, they camped near the mouth of the canyon leading to the strange area. We discovered this when one pointed to their campsite on his map.

While relaxing one evening, after a long, tiring search for this elusive treasure, they heard a sound like rain hitting the tent. Stepping outside, they saw the sky was clear. All at once a shower of hundreds of small stones came cascading down around them. Most were the size of a large pea, were reddish brown and resembled hematite, which is an iron ore.

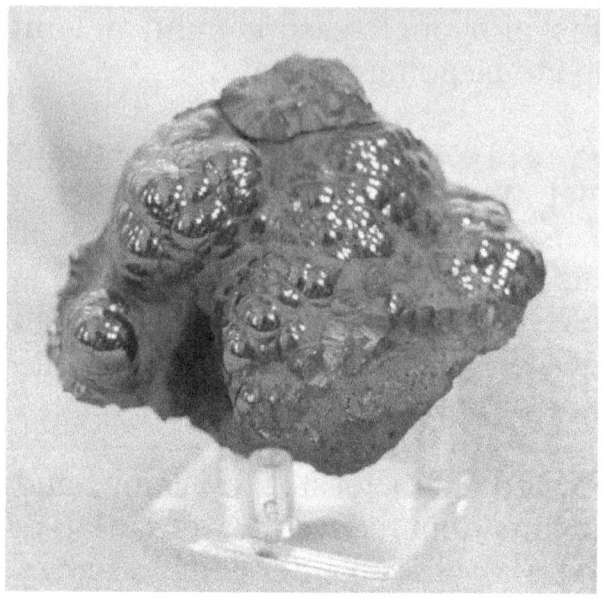

Picking several up, they noticed they were quite warm to the touch. Since their camp wasn't located near any high cliffs, they had no idea where the stones could have originated. George, a member of the group, jokingly said: "Perhaps we're camping on some ancient Indian burial ground, and the spirits want us to leave." Of course, he wasn't quite serious, but it did remind him of an article he had read about a similar incident occurring on burial grounds somewhere in the Midwest.

However, by now, one has to admit something

quite out of the ordinary encircles this strange site. I won't definitely say their encounter with the warm stones had anything to do with our odd out-of-time region; but Indian spirits or not, something weird occurred while they sat relaxing in their tent."

Bizarre Treasure Hunt

"After our two-year adventure ended without finding buried gold or lost mines, we returned to Washington State for almost a year. We then moved to Arizona, making Tucson our home.

Most of our adult lives have been one long adventure after the other. If Roy and Walt arrived at our door with some wild treasure lead, we'd be off with them the next day. To live such a lifestyle, we all remained single. We were one big happy family of devil-may-care adventurers.

The strange occurrence Quinn experienced on Oct. 14, 1973.

"During one of our two-week adventures, I found myself near the canyon that leads towards that oddball site. Not having been there in almost four years, I decided to pay it a visit. The canyon was just as rugged as ever. After climbing and slipping among the boulders, I finally arrived at the steep hill leading to the site above.

It's a long, weary climb, so I paused for a breather half way up. I sat on the slope facing north. Too my left (west) was the steep hill that followed the canyon, perhaps a mile; but something was definitely wrong. Below, and to my left, was a canyon, where none had previously existed. Curious, I made my way down, entering it from the eastside, so I thought.

However, I soon discovered that I was in the same canyon that led toward the hill that I had just scaled; but I was more than 250 yards back down the canyon on a different slope and now facing south. Somehow, I had mysteriously been transported to the new location. Thinking I was looking west, I was really looking east seeing the canyon I had just hiked.

There is no way on earth that I could have reached this other slope while climbing the original hill. Realizing where I was, I suddenly knew why this had happened. Any remaining skepticism I might have had about this crazy site *vanished* – never to return!

Although apprehensive about continuing, and knowing I should have departed the area immediately – curiosity make me push on, making my way through the grueling climb once again, eventually passing the spot – where minutes before I had been resting.

The hair stood up on the back of my neck, realizing that if something within this site had caused my teleportation, it might have landed me in another time, as well. What a frightening though – it overwhelmed me; but I knew I had to keep my cool to get out of there.

Soon, I arrived back at the beginning of the site, turned and looked around. To my delight (and surprise) everything appeared perfectly normal. No shimmering effects, lights or other odd observations were made. However, in standing there, I noticed how silent it was – not a breeze, a birdcall, nothing! Looking down, I saw the hairs on my arms standing straight up, like when you're near static electricity. I don't know why, exactly, but I began feeling uneasy, and decided to leave.

For what it's worth, it seemed that each time we visited this Arizona Twilight Zone, we'd discover another geological oddity (anomaly), and this time was no different.

While descending the hill, I found an outcropping of thunder eggs: a cryo-crystalline variety of quartz found in egg-shaped nodules. We had searched this area before, and I couldn't understand how we had missed seeing them; so I gathered a few and continued on.

If what happened *was* caused by this tricky, mysterious region, I didn't want to, perhaps, get zapped a second time, and wind up – God knows where. You can imagine (when climbing out of that canyon) how relieved I was to find my jeep waiting for me – exactly where I'd left it three hours earlier.

Glancing skyward, I spotted a jet passing overhead. I was sure happy it wasn't some prehistoric bird. Of course, I can joke about it now, but always in the back of my mind is the knowledge that something serious could have occurred while I was in the presence of that weird, upside-down area.

At camp that evening, I tried to arrive at some satisfactory answers. Some force could have been released from the area, but being well below the site, I didn't receive its full impact. Anyway, something moved me within a microsecond without ever realizing it – until I found myself on the other side. Believe what you will, but this wasn't my imagination.

I've kept the location of this strange place a secret – all these years, because I don't want the area turning into a circus sideshow; or run the risk of someone getting hurt. Sometimes I'm tempted to map the location, for fear of someone happening upon it and disappearing – but then think better against it. I'll just have to live with the chance; after all – the locals know where it is – and they're not talking, either.

Only five of my living friends know its location. The others, Roy, Walt, and Louie – have gone to that Big Desert in the sky, where we'll meet again someday. It's not like it's some UFO landing site, or mythical place to communicate with spirits from beyond; I don't know what it is, but I do know that it's capable of altering time at will – and should be left alone.

On my last visit to this wondrous place, I discovered the top portion of the archway had collapsed. All that remains are the two columns. Will this damage interfere with its ability to change time? The following story answers that question."

Two New Friends

Quinn recalls: "During 2001, my friend Bill R. and his wife, Mary, wanted to visit the area after hearing the remarkable stories surrounding it. (Both promised not to reveal its location to others.) Even so, showing them the rugged route on a map, it still took them several attempts to find it.

During their first attempt to reach this forbidden zone, Bill injured his knee, but managed to continue. I had to remind them how unfriendly this region can be while prowling its harsh domain, and urged them to be cautious.

On their second trip, they missed the right hill; however, they did discover a portion of the geode bed, and were amazed by its size. That evening, while camping within the canyon, both claimed a slight vibration came from the nearby geodes, when placing their hands upon them. Mary later mentioned that it was a spooky place, and she felt uneasy throughout the whole night.

While exploring the following morning, Bill discovered a hollow geode that was large enough to sit in. I found that odd, because we didn't find a geode anywhere near that large while we were there; and none, even remotely that large, of the more than ten times I was there.

Like I've mentioned, it's a real odd place: you see something one time – and it's gone the next. Makes me wonder if these geodes could be the main source that activates the natural energy within the area, or if that's just more wild, unfounded speculation?

On their final trip into this 'never-never land' of mystery, Bill and Mary found the correct hill. After an exhausting climb, they arrived at the site. Even though Bill found most of what I told him to search for, the archway eluded them.

While searching, Bill and Mary spotted what resembled the two columns off in the distance; but upon arriving at the site, both columns had vanished. Was this their imagination, a mirage incident, or were the strange forces within the area playing with their minds?

After spending the day searching and not witnessing any strange activities, except for the vanishing columns, they decided to leave, arriving at their truck after dark. While preparing to leave, following their tracks out to the ranch road, Bill glanced toward the canyon. In the sky above the site, he reported seeing a circular transparent donut-shaped glow, resembling the Aurora Borealis. From the inside rim, tiny sparkling particles were observed cascading downward. Bill grabbed his digital camera and took a few shots, before it vanished as mysteriously as it appeared.

However, later that night, only the black sky and moon appeared in the photo; but when using a magnifying glass, you can see something else that's just too faint to make out.

Mary refuses to go there anymore."

Fact or Fiction?

What we have out there may be a natural phenomena (created accidentally by nature) or perhaps not. Whatever it is, it alters time, and there's no way to predict when this might occur.

The majority of these tricks of time seem to occur during the summer, and winter storm season, when lots of energy is about; while others happen during the stillness of the night, or on sunny days.

Undoubtedly, there will be skeptics and believers; but this is definitely not a hoax or a figment of this writer's imagination. Such a place exists – high on a plateau near the Mexican border, and odd things *do occur* at random within its mysterious boundaries."

Can this site alter time? Quinn believes so – until he is proven wrong.

Strange activities no doubt still occur near this bewildering location, but go unnoticed by human eyes due to its remote proximity to civilization. Quinn says that there is no doubt in his mind that he will return there again one day. *We wish him luck!*

Will this uncanny mystery ever be solved? Only time will tell. Quinn believes that there's ample evidence to support the claim that something quite unnatural happens at random within this place.

Whatever you believe – what's that old saying: that "truth is stranger than fiction"? If ever that rang true – it rings true, now.

◇◇◇

Not There

by

Lyn Murray

<u>Things that go *Poof* in plain sight*!*</u>

This section explores people, places and things that – one minute are there, and the next . . . *are not.*

98

Lost in Yantis

A personal experience.

It's 2008. I'm making a run to Marshall, Texas to visit relatives, and cut through a small town called Yantis. Now, when I say Yantis is small – I mean it's small. They have one streetlight at the main intersection that leads to other, more recognizable municipalities. *That's it.*

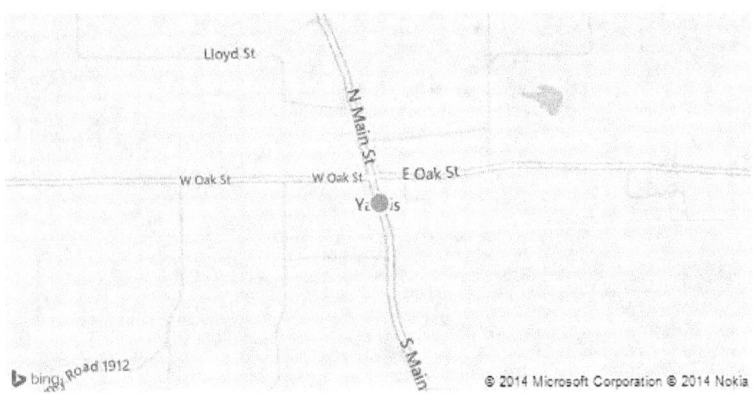

As of the census of 2000, there were 321 souls, 144 households, and 84 families residing in the town.

However, this isn't meant to say that Yantis doesn't have a lot going on. For a small Texas town – they're in the know. At this main intersection (State Highway 154 & FM Road 17 – or Main and Oak) you'll find whatever you need: a great Cafe (good eats), meat market and Steak House, Food Mart (gas and more); and a little up the road you'll even find a Dollar General; and if you want to stay the night, their are some Scenic Cabins that have you covered!

I love going through Yantis (you'll find some of the friendliest folks on Earth there) that's why I find a way to pass through every chance I get. So, no, this was not my first time here. However, on this day I was in a hurry, didn't have time to stop, so when I got to the light, rather than continuing on my usual path, I turned left. *No problem.* The street was clearly marked and pointing the way. Or so I thought.

I don't know what it was, exactly, but about ten minutes into my drive I felt lost. The optimal word here being "felt". Suddenly nothing felt right. I'm sure you know the feeling. Everything looks right, the signs are correct, the arrows point in the right direction – but North feels South, and West feels East. But it's more than a feeling of being turned around (which I considered), something wasn't right.

The signs said that I was going in the right direction, but it *felt* wrong, so I turned and went in the opposite direction, until I found myself back where I started. Which was impossible, because I hadn't made a circle.

So allowing the car idle at the red light, and taking a moment to collect myself, I turned left again. Just as before – everything indicated that I was going in the right direction, but it still *"felt"* wrong.

Eventually, I ended back at the intersection – just as before. This circling scenario happened four times before I decided to pull into the gas station and ask for help. The officer there was kind enough to lead me out of town, and see me safely on my way.

The odd thing is – when he led me out of town, he led me the exact same way I had headed out on my own. The exact same way! The signs were all the same, the arrows were the same: North was North, and South was South – but the feeling of heading in the wrong direction was gone. *Completely gone!*

I have asked myself many times if I could have just been turned around? It's easy enough to get turned around when you are in unfamiliar surroundings. I've really considered that possibility, and I would like to say that was it – *but I can't!*

I can't, because I know myself. Most of my adult life has been spent in cars traveling from place to place. I know how to navigate strange terrain. I know to *trust* signs. This was different. I wasn't lost on the road – I was lost in time. Space and time had somehow been altered. The electromagnetics of the place had changed. An alternate reality, perhaps? *Perhaps.* Whatever it was, wherever I was, the two realities eventually converged and aligned themselves with "my normal", and time (as I knew it) returned to normal.

I knew not to panic, because this was not my first time experiencing similar phenomena. Some believe that all of us experience time shifts (anomalies) all the time, but that few ever realize it. If this is true – then we (all of us) are in some way – time travelers.

That's one possibility, here's another: could invisible wormholes, gateways – whatever you want to call them, suddenly manifest and interfere with our perception of reality? Could there be certain regions prone to such anomalies? Of course there are. Could Yantis sit in one of these regions? If it does, the residents may or may not be aware of anything unusual. Time displacement is a funny thing – sometimes it takes an outsider to notice peculiarities.

Interesting concept, isn't it.

Wormholes on Earth?

"According to a group of mathematicians, it may be possible to create devices with internal tunnels that are invisible to detection by electromagnetic waves—wormholes, in a sense." *So – there you have it!*

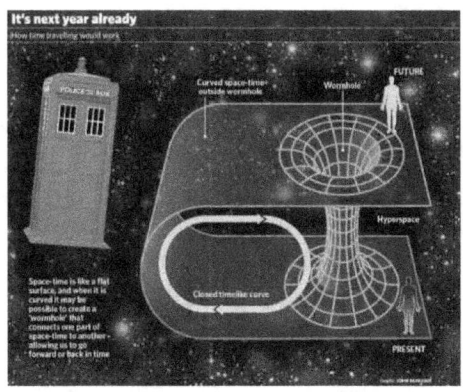

Whistle-stop Inn

Big Sandy, Texas

It all began in 2005. Big Sandy, Texas, as you can see from the map, sits dead center of U. S. Highway 80 – a major thoroughfare headed somewhere else!

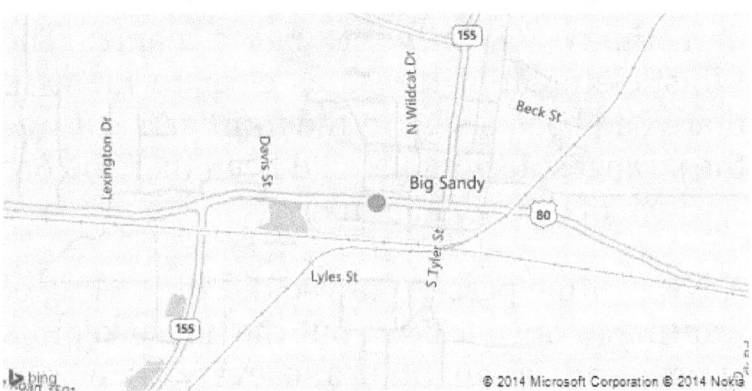

It's not that Big Sandy isn't beautiful (as small Texas towns go) it's a lovely place; but like most small towns, to anyone but residents, it is a place to pass through on your way to somewhere else.

Not if they knew what I know! Which they will after I tell this story.

The railroad passes through this town, and on the south side of the tracks sits a large two story house that my husband and I had once considered buying. It wasn't for sale – but that didn't seem to bother us.

I have often fancied running a B&B (Bed and Breakfast) and thought this home would make the perfect site. It came with a name. I mean, immediately. Mind you, it didn't have a name (it was a residence) but upon seeing it for the first time – I knew it had a name: The Whistle-stop Inn. It was as clear to me as if there had been a sign in the front yard. It was the strangest feeling, like I'd been there before – which of course, I hadn't.

Anyway, time passed, and so did the feeling of wanting to open a B&B, but the house kept its appeal and fascination, and every time we'd come anywhere near Big Sandy, we'd stop by the house – like you would drop by and say Hi to an old friend. So odd!

However, on one of our trips we were saddened to find that the house had been torn down. We were both upset, but it just broke my heart! We had a connection – the house and I.

Tearfully we drove back across the tracks for the last time, and headed for the corner gas station for a coke before heading home. After checking out and pulling away from the station, we stopped to take one last look at the dream that almost was – only to find the house intact!

You can imagine our frame of mind. Startled doesn't even come close.

We couldn't believe our eyes, and immediately turned around, heading back up the street toward the house. After crossing the railroad track, we drove up to the house, parked out front, and just sat there like two lost souls, before circling the block to do it all over again. We must have repeated this scenario five or six times before deciding to go home.

The following week, I had some business in a nearby town (about 30 or so miles from Big Sandy) so I decided to drop by the house for a visit.

It was gone! I mean, not a board, foundation, nothing at all to even indicate that there had once been a house in that location! I was so shaken by the experience that I found it hard to move, but eventually I continued onto my appointment, and tried to put the incident behind me, chalking it up to – 'just one of those things'!

After the meeting, I just went home, and wouldn't pass through Big Sandy again for another three months. But when I did, I was in for the shock of my life – the house was back!

On occasion, I still pass that way, and I'm always drawn back to the house. Sometimes it's there – and sometimes it isn't. An acquaintance thinks that because this is not my first experience with missing people, places and things – that I'm the one who's disappearing, shifting, passing from one reality into another. Some form of *Bilocation?*

I don't mind telling you – that *unsettles* me. How can I not know that I'm experiencing dimensional shifts, rifts in time? You'd think there'd be nausea, or dizziness – *something?* It's possible that the realities to which I'm traveling are so similar that the shift is undetectable. Maybe, but then how do you explain my husband's experience? After all, he was with me the first time this anomaly occurred. *Shared psychosis?* What could it all mean? Are the people in my life also traveling through time? Some speculate (because we can't know for sure) that we all – from time to time, pass from one existence to another. Just how close to reality was the series – *Sliders*. Makes me think. If this is really happening, and I'm not suffering major psychotic episodes – who knows?! *I surely don't!*

Next week – I drop by the house again. I can't stay away. My husband doesn't go with me anymore; he says . . . *he doesn't want to know.*

112

Into Thin Air

Vanished

People disappear every day. It's been estimated that as many as 10 million people are reported missing each year in the U.S. alone; about 95 percent of them return, or are otherwise accounted for. Of the remaining 5 percent, some are runaways, others are kidnappings, abductions, or the victims of some other crime.

There is a small percentage of disappearances, however, for which there is no easy explanation. The fate of these people, sometimes groups of people, is left for us to wonder about. Did they unwittingly step into a time portal? Were they swallowed up by a rift in our three-dimensional world? Were they abducted by extraterrestrials in UFOs? These are pretty far-out suggestions, to be sure, but the circumstances of the following unexplained disappearances leave us scratching our heads in bewilderment.

Case 1:

TIME TUNNEL

In 1975, a man named Jackson Wright was driving with his wife from New Jersey to New York City. This required them to travel through the Lincoln Tunnel. According to Wright, who was driving, once through the tunnel he pulled the car over to wipe the windshield of condensation. His wife Martha volunteered to clean off the back window so they could more readily resume their trip. When Wright turned around, his wife was gone. He neither heard nor saw anything unusual take place, and a subsequent investigation could find no evidence of foul play. Martha Wright had just disappeared.

Case 2:

THE MYSTERIOUS CLOUD

Three soldiers claimed to be witnesses to the bizarre disappearance of an entire battalion in 1915. They finally came forward with the strange story 50 years after the infamous Gallipoli campaign of WWI. The three members of a New Zealand field company said they watched from a clear vantage point as a battalion of the Royal Norfolk Regiment marched up a hillside in Suvla Bay, Turkey. The hill was shrouded in a low-lying cloud that the English soldiers marched straight into without hesitation.

They never came out. After the last of the battalion had entered the cloud, it slowly lifted off the hillside to join other clouds in the sky. When the war was over, figuring the battalion had been captured and held prisoner, the British government demanded that Turkey return them. The Turks insisted, however, that it had neither captured not made contact with these English soldiers.

Case 3:

THE STONEHENGE DISAPPEARANCES

The mysterious standing stones of Stonehenge in England was the site of an amazing disappearance in August, 1971. At this time Stonehenge was not yet protected from the public, and on this particular night, a group of "hippies" decided to pitch tents in the center of the circle and spend the night. They built a campfire, lit several joints of pot and sat around smoking and signing. Their campout was abruptly interrupted at about 2 a.m. by a severe thunder storm that quickly blew in over Salisbury Plain.

Bright bolts of lightning crashed down on the area, striking area trees and even the standing stones themselves. Two witnesses, a farmer and a policeman, said that the stones of the ancient monument lit up with an eerie blue light that was so intense that they had to avert their eyes. They heard screams from the campers and the two witnesses rushed to the scene expecting to find injured -- or even dead -- campers. To their surprise, they found no one. All that remained within the circle of stones were several smoldering tent pegs and the drowned remains of a campfire. The hippies themselves were gone without a trace.

Case 4:

THE BENNINGTON TRIANGLE

Between 1920 and 1950, Bennington, Vermont was the site of several completely unexplained disappearances:

- **On December 1, 1949, Mr. Tetford vanished from a crowded bus.** Tetford was on his way home to Bennington from a trip to St. Albans, Vermont. Tetford, an ex-soldier who lived in the Soldier's Home in Bennington, was sitting on the bus with 14 other passengers. They all testified to seeing him there, sleeping in his seat. When the bus reached its destination, however, Tetford was gone, although his belongings were still on the luggage rack and a bus timetable lay open on his empty seat. Tetford has never returned or been found.
- **On December 1, 1946, an 18-year-old student named Paula Welden vanished while taking a walk.** Welden was walking along the Long Trail into Glastonbury Mountain. She was seen by a middle-aged couple that was strolling about 100 yards behind her. They lost sight of her when she followed the trail around a rocky outcropping, but when they rounded the outcropping themselves, she was nowhere to be seen. Welden has not been seen nor heard from since.
- **In mid-October, 1950, 8-year old Paul Jepson disappeared from a**

farm. Paul's mother, who earned a living as an animal caretaker, left her small son happily playing near a pig sty while she tended to the animals. A short time later, she returned to find him missing. An extensive search of the area proved fruitless.

- THE VANISHED HANDICAPPED MAN
- **Owen Parfitt had been paralyzed by a massive stroke.** In June, 1763 in Shepton Mallet, England, Parfitt sat outside his sister's home, as was often his habit on warm evenings. Virtually unable to move, the 60-year-old man sat quietly is his nightshirt upon his folded greatcoat. Across the road was a farm where workers were finishing their workday by pooking the hay.
- At about 7 p.m., Parfitt's sister, Susannah, went outside with a neighbor to help Parfitt move back into the house, as a storm was approaching. But he was gone. Only his folded greatcoat upon which he sat remained. Investigations of this mysterious disappearance were carried out as late as 1933, but no trace or clues to Parfitt's fate were ever uncovered.
- **THE DISAPPEARING DIPLOMAT**

- **British diplomat Benjamin Bathurst vanished into thin air in 1809.** Bathurst was returning to Hamburg with a companion after a mission to the Austrian court. Along the way, they had stopped for dinner at an inn in the town of Perelberg. Upon finishing the meal, they returned to their waiting horse-drawn coach. Bathurst's companion watched as the diplomat stepped over to the front of the coach to examine to horses -- and simply vanished without a trace.

Case 5:

Virginia Dare

As the first child born to English parents in the New World, Virginia Dare became a poster child for early American colonialism following her birth in 1587. Her family was part of just 120 Englishmen and -women to settle on Roanoke Island, off the coast of what is now North Carolina. The colony's governor — and Virginia's grandfather — left for England soon after she was born to secure more financial and material resources for the foundering settlement. When he finally returned three years later, he couldn't find a trace of the toddler — or any of the other settlers. Only one clue remained: the word *Croatan* had been carved on one of the settlement's posts, leading many to believe that the Native American Croatan tribe had kidnapped or killed the settlers. Roanoke Island became known as the Lost Colony.

Case 6:

Ambrose Bierce (Author)

In October 1913 Bierce, then aged 71, departed Washington, D.C., for a tour of his old Civil War battlefields. By December, he had passed through Louisiana and Texas, crossing by way of El Paso into Mexico, which was in the throes of revolution. In Ciudad Juárez, he joined Poncho Villa's army as an observer, and in that role, he witnessed the Battle of Tierra Blanca.

Bierce is known to have accompanied Villa's army as far as the city of Chihuahua. His last known communication with the world was a letter he wrote there to Blanche Partington, a close friend, dated December 26, 1913. [14][15] After closing this letter by saying, "As to me, I leave here tomorrow for an unknown destination," he vanished without a trace, his disappearance becoming one of the most famous in American literary history. Skeptic Joe Nickell argued that no letter had ever been found; all that existed was a notebook belonging to his secretary and companion, Carrie Christiansen, containing a rough summary of a purported letter and her statement that the originals had been destroyed.

Oral tradition in Sierra Mojada, Coahuila, documented by the priest James Lienert, states that Bierce was executed by firing squad in the town cemetery there. Again, Nickell finds this story to be rather incredible. He quotes Bierce's friend and biographer Walter Neale as saying that in 1913, Bierce had not ridden for quite some time, was suffering from serious asthma, and had been severely critical of Poncho Villa. Neale concludes that it would have been highly unlikely for Bierce to have gone to Mexico and joined up with Villa.

All investigations into his fate have proven fruitless, and Nickell concedes that despite a lack of hard evidence that Bierce had gone to Mexico, there is also none that he had not. Therefore, despite an abundance of theories (including death by suicide), his end remains shrouded in mystery.

NASA Fesses Up?!

A favorite theme of science fiction is "the portal"--an extraordinary opening in space or time that connects travelers to distant realms. A good portal is a shortcut, a guide, a door into the unknown. If only they actually existed....

It turns out that they do, sort of, and a NASA-funded researcher at the University of Iowa has figured out how to find them.

"We call them X-points or electron diffusion regions," explains plasma physicist Jack Scudder of the University of Iowa. "They're places where the magnetic field of Earth connects to the magnetic field of the Sun, creating an uninterrupted path leading from our own planet to the sun's atmosphere 93 million miles away."

Observations by NASA's THEMIS spacecraft and Europe's Cluster probes suggest that these magnetic portals open and close dozens of times each day. They're typically located a few tens of thousands of kilometers from Earth where the geomagnetic field meets the onrushing solar wind. Most portals are small and short-lived; others are yawning, vast, and sustained. Tons of energetic particles can flow through the openings, heating Earth's upper atmosphere, sparking geomagnetic storms, and igniting bright polar auroras.

NASA is planning a mission called "MMS," short for Magnetospheric Multiscale Mission, due to launch in 2014, to study the phenomenon. Bristling with energetic particle detectors and magnetic sensors, the four spacecraft of MMS will spread out in Earth's magnetosphere and surround the portals to observe how they work.

Just one problem: Finding them. Magnetic portals are invisible, unstable, and elusive. They open and close without warning "and there are no signposts to guide us in," notes Scudder.

Actually, there are signposts, and Scudder has found them.

Portals form via the process of magnetic reconnection. Mingling lines of magnetic force from the sun and Earth criss-cross and join to create the openings. "X-points" are where the criss-cross takes place. The sudden joining of magnetic fields can propel jets of charged particles from the X-point, creating an "electron diffusion region."

To learn how to pinpoint these events, Scudder looked at data from a space probe that orbited Earth more than 10 years ago.

"In the late 1990s, NASA's Polar spacecraft spent years in Earth's magnetosphere," explains Scudder, "and it encountered many X-points during its mission."

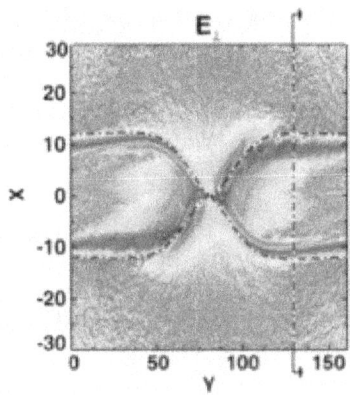

Data from NASA's Polar spacecraft, circa 1998, provided crucial clues to finding magnetic X-points.

Image Credit: NASA

Because Polar carried sensors similar to those of MMS, Scudder decided to see how an X-point looked to Polar. "Using Polar data, we have found five simple combinations of magnetic field and energetic particle measurements that tell us when we've come across an X-point or an electron diffusion region. A single spacecraft, properly instrumented, can make these measurements."

This means that single member of the MMS constellation using the diagnostics can find a portal and alert other members of the constellation. Mission planners long thought that MMS might have to spend a year or so learning to find portals before it could study them. Scudder's work short cuts the process, allowing MMS to get to work without delay.

It's a shortcut worthy of the best portals of fiction, only this time the portals are real. And with the new "signposts" we know how to find them.

Metaphysical Transportation

(Trans-Portals' Theory)

Energy Gates in Space and Time

Those keynote events, which recently awakened your planet to faith and to action, have torn away the last veils of denial from the Collective Consciousness. A stone has been thrown into the water, and ripples of pure energy now spread around the globe--- ushering in what will eventually become known as The Age of Conscious Choice. Doorways are opening, and magic is afoot! This is no longer a game to be played by just the spiritual elite. What was once a privilege of the chosen few now becomes the heritage of all.

All around you, in every place, there exist Energy Gates---portals in time and space--- through which a person can pass to new life and experiences. Some are visible, and some are of the mind and heart. All of them are real. Some portals exist as specific places. Simply to visit these locations is to be transformed. Other portals require energetic "passwords" or "vibratory signatures" to activate them. Still others--- those connected to the highest levels of transformation --- require passwords, along with "sponsorship" by an Etheric Guide, so that the unconscious or unprepared can not enter them unaware.

There are many kinds of Trans-Portals. Most are opened through the verbalization of some goal or desire for personal development. In such cases, the INTENT of the traveler becomes a blade that cuts an opening in the Veil which divides the universes. Once a portal is opened, your journey begins. A vortex draws the individual in, and certain "changes" are effected, so that transport to an adjacent universe can occur.

JOURNEYS THROUGH TIME

AND SPACE THEORIES

Transformation begins with two elements:
Disorder and Disintegration.

When a physical body passes through a portal, it begins to be broken down into basic elements that can be transported easily within the Multiverse. Once a decision is made, this process is usually so rapid that it is barely noticeable. The human mind has a tremendous filtration ability, and has a habit of editing out all knowledge concerning what's being here. The mind's power to knit together universes, into a logical sequence, gives a person the impression that reality is one continuous landscape, rather than the infinite collation of alternative possibilities, which it can be.

The arrival of disorder ("chaos energy") into any organized structure produces CONFUSION. If you examine this word, you will see that it is composed of "con," which means "against" and "fusion," that which binds physical material together. To become con-fused means to LIFT OFF from your current orientation, in the same way a rocket ship launches, and moves towards something new.

Confusion scrambles the mind. It mixes and mingles old orientations, to clear the way for new ones. Its physical counterpart is CONSUMPTION. When a Trans-Portal is entered, the energy acceleration actually consumes the physical body. Once the traveler arrives at his new destination, the original INTENT manifests, and down steps itself into an appropriate physical vehicle. .

Once a person has arrived at a destination point, his mind is free to concoct any number of rationalizations to explain why and how he is there, rather than where he was. Sometimes, it will appear as though he awakens from sleep, only to assume that he must have been dreaming. At other times, he will tell himself that he has experienced "time loss" during a car trip, or while working in the back yard. And in some cases, the shift is so drastic, and the internal weaving of universes so pristine, that the individual never realizes he has moved at all.

You would be quite surprised to know how many fantastic journeys you have taken---only to file them, forget about them, and resume working at some mundane task . . . .as though nothing had happened to you. Rest assured, your "travel photos" are all kept safe and available, waiting for the time when you will review and enjoy them again . . . a time that is rapidly approaching, by the way!

ENERGY GATE THEORIES

What is an Energy Gate? Basically, it is the intersection of desire and opportunity – wherein the signature vibration of a person synchronizes itself with physical conditions to produce a change or an effect. Another expression that has often been used to describe it is "a window of opportunity."

Energy Gates, themselves, can be physical in form, or they can exist merely as states of mind. Once inside, all the rules that existed "over there" seem not to apply to what's happening "here." Passing through Energy Gates, mothers and fathers have transformed themselves, so as to be able to perform super-human powers in order to save their children from harm. Then, having passed back through, these folks were amazed at what "had come over them," and what they had been able to accomplish.

Lovers have faced impossible odds, and overcome great obstacles in order to be together. The activation key is their desire, and their power is nurtured by that for which they would rather die than live without. This is also the sourcing of power for heroes and tyrants alike. Energy knows no moral champion, save the person who is willing to give up anything and everything in order to achieve a goal---to move from where he is to become part of something new. Of course, as an aside . . . today's "solution" may end up being tomorrow's "problem," but that can be dealt with when the time comes.

Some of your most famous and powerful spots on the planet are Energy Gates. For example, your Stonehenge, with its many stone formations that are stacked to symbolize doors and archways. They are inspirational, and they teach that the possibilities which surround you are infinite indeed.

Yesterday's warriors and explorers have left you a rich legacy which you can study and celebrate. However, you must also remember that today is your day. Once you have created your own transformations and miracles, you, too, can put up memorials and stones – leaving a bit of your legacy for those who will come after.

ELEVATORS OF THE MULTIVERSE THEORIES

Transport between dimensions can be horizontal (through time), vertical (density to density), or diagonal (variations of both). Whenever a traveler begins a journey, it will always manifest full circle, to return to its point of origin. Stops along the way may be recorded to memory, within an individual life, as though they represented an end. But really, there is no end. Everything moves in a circle. Any appearance of an "end" is illusion, and a powerful illusion it can be! Lessons are learned, and the wheel of life continues to turn.

There are many ancient structures which have served, in days past, as human "Ascension Chambers." One such structure is older than Stonehenge, and exists now in Ireland. It is called Newgrange. Inside, the passageway is rounded at the top. Underneath the main floor is a giant crystal, which energizes and facilitates all who enter to make whatever Multiversal Leaps their hearts desire.

Another Elevator Gateway is well-known as The Great Pyramid in Egypt. Down through history, this particular Trans-Portal

has been a favorite access point for Atlanteans (among others) who have done experimentation with time travel and who still use it for comings and goings today.

These famous structures are mere examples of the manifold Elevators that exist all around you. They are famous, filled with tourists, and are protected because of their notoriety. Others are less known, and are points of interest to those among you who are serious about your journeys, and wish not to be disturbed in your process. Gates can be opened, and Gates can be sealed again. It is all a matter of mutual contract between a traveler and the reality context within which he moves.

PAYING FOR THE RIDE

In high-rise office buildings, you get to ride the elevators for free. They are made of steel and granite, and their destinations consist of floors, stacked systematically, one upon the other. In the Multiverse, the ascension process happens a bit differently. Instead of changing ALTITUDE, a rider in the Multiverse changes ATTITUDE.

Each universe exists somewhat like a filmstrip which passes through a projector at variable speeds (densities). When you change the speed of a filmstrip, the pictures contained thereon will seem to change as well. When a person incarnates, his mind is his projector . . . and his entire perceptual universe becomes his screen. As his vibration rises and falls, the images on the screen become light or dark, sinister or playful, all in accordance to the pitch at which his perception is tuned.

The highest level of knowledge and expression, all interpretations are neutral. In other words, there is room for everything, and everyone has a place at the dinner table. To label something as "good" or "evil" is to place it within a polarity, which stops its expansion. When a person becomes invested in a list of definitions (i.e. when he creates a belief system) . . . he, too, solidifies . . . and commits himself to the life process that is playing itself out at that frequency of vibration. There is nothing wrong with this, people do it everyday.

▼

GETTING ON THE ELEVATOR

Assuming an attitude of unconditional acceptance, or neutrality becomes an AUTOMATIC ELEVATOR within the Multiverse, enabling any of you to move freely between the various realities that exist within All That Is. To decrease vibration, it is necessary to form a judgment concerning the universe you are inhabiting. The degree of deceleration is correspondent to the intensity and essential inflexibility in the attitude of the observer. The more absolute the judgment, the heavier the reality becomes. If a person believes that something is very, very bad he will live within a context of fear concerning its presence in his reality. If he believes that something is very, very good---he will still live in fear, as he will dread losing it.

Different Polarities – same vibration. Neutrality is the doorway out of any universe.

When a person lets go of judgments (self and others), the elevator moves up. When he takes new ones up again, the elevator goes down. If he remains constant, he has the option of getting off and doing business at any "floor" that matches his energy. These are the laws that govern movement within the Multiverse. You have been using them skillfully and constantly from the beginning of your journey here. However, now you have the option of using them consciously to intensify the power of your experience.

FINDING A STATE OF NEUTRALITY

If freedom within the Multiverse depends upon Neutrality, you may find it helpful to know some essential facts about how this crucial component is lost and how to find it again.

Whether he realizes it or not, in order to attain and hold himself within an attitude of judgment, each traveler (or projector) carries within him a "scale of evaluation," somewhat like the one being held by the Archetype, Lady Justice. One side of the scale is loaded down with what he believes to be "facts" about the universe in which he exists. On the other scale, "evidence" is accrued to contradict the basic premises which he holds sacred.

This basic conflict produces a vibrational momentum which feeds the development of each particular universe.

As the scales shift, the emotions in that universe will shift with them. Drama, intrigue, and outright comedy will frequently be the result. An attractive package to invite a person to stay there, wouldn't you say?

All truth is relative to the context within which it is viewed. Since there are universes, within the Multiverse, that honor each and every belief – the issue of what is "true" or not is dependent entirely on where a person wishes to go, and what experiences he requires to complete his soul's evolution. Therefore, to achieve a state of Neutrality--all a traveler must do is to return to his Scales of Evaluation and rearrange his "facts."

Each universe contains its own intrinsic "evidence" to support the basic premises

142

around which it functions. By introducing "new evidence" to old belief systems, the flow of emotion can turn, bringing the entire vibrational density back to "zero point." Once the attachments are cleared, the traveler is freed to go anywhere (or any when) he desires to go.

CONSUMED BY DOUBT –

DISEASED BY HESITATION

As a necessary process for transporting oneself throughout the Multiverse. Do you know that "consumption" is also a word that has been applied to many disease processes, which have existed down through history?

This outlines how Trans-Portals are formed. It is focused INTENT that cuts an opening in the Veil, and it is DESIRE which draws a person through that portal to be transformed. However, if the transition process becomes interrupted – if a traveler doesn't hurry through and complete his process, some negative consequences can result.

Those conditions which are called "disease," within your society, are produced within your gateways to transformation. The changes have not been completed, that is why there is pain. It matters not what type of disease we are discussing. They are all simply doorways, into which individuals have ventured. For whatever reason, these folks get stuck – halfway in and halfway out – and they become disoriented and hesitate to finish their transition. The specific symptoms of the disease are determined by which parts of the body have been inserted into the portal, and which are held back.

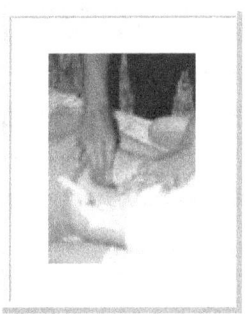

The deterioration or weakening which makes up a disease state comes from the decomposition process which occurs in order to teleport a traveler from "here to there," where he is reformed again. The change is meant to be instantaneous and complete – which it is, if a person fully steps through the portal. But if he hesitates, if the blade on his "scalpel" of decision is dull or halting, he or she can become stuck in the Gate. It is only when he realizes what he is doing, and what he really wants, that the process can be restored, and his journey completed.

At the most basic level, the only "healing" that is ever needed is awareness. This cannot emphasize this enough. The basic adage of "know thyself" is foundational to all growth and attainment. Once a person has achieved that, the next most important lesson is "pay attention to what is happening to you." The final task is to make a decision. Sometimes, refusing to decide is a decision. Be conscious rather than unconscious.

This is a New Millennium! Make some mistakes now, won't you? It will be all right. Life is a risk. Be willing to play with it a bit.

You simply need to ask, open, and wait. Do not become attached to a form concerning how all of this will look. Each life itinerary is different. Each manifestation of Reconnection is unique to the individual and to his or her situation. So let it be!

You, as a planet, are only beginning to grasp the enormity of your life's potential. In your own way and in your own timing, you will finally discover that you are truly limitless. When you do, there will be the wondrous joy of RIDING THAT INFINITY, like a surfboard, as well as forming it and shaping it in your hands. But for now, let those hands open to receive again what was yours---knowledge, ability, and the wisdom to integrate and use it to your advantage.

Ancient Time Portals

On September 26, 1905 in Bern, Switzerland, Albert Einstein published his special theory of relativity. According to his astonishing scientific breakthrough, space and time are one, opening the page for many questions such as: "time travel, a possibility?"

In the old theory of Newton, space was a rigid container, and time was an absolute flow while in Einstein's theory, this was revolutionized. Space now became a flexible medium, and time could now be altered. Einstein realized that if you move faster, the ticks on your clock actually change. Prior to Einstein, no one understood that or would even have expected that, because it only happens when you get very, very close to the speed of light. There is a way within the laws of physics to travel long distances and still be alive, and that actually is related to special relativity and the idea that if you can travel very, very close to the speed of light, time will slow down for you. And in this sense, if you could travel very near the speed of light, only a day or two would pass, instead of the whole four years.

What we find interesting is that through out our history, there are said to be many more tales of time travel some of them dating back hundreds or thousands of years.

In the popular TV series Ancient Aliens, Erick von Daniken states that there is evidence of time travel found in the Bible (actually, it's found in forbidden religious text, text that didn't make it into the Bible, but here's the quote: (paraphrased) "In this text, the prophet Jeremiah was sitting together with a few of his friends, and there was a young boy. His name was Abimelech, and Jeremiah said to Abimelech, "Go out of Jerusalem, there is a hill and collect some figs for us." The boy went out and collected the fresh figs. All of a sudden, Abimelech hears some noise and wind in the air, and he becomes unconscious, he had a blackout. After a time he wakes up again, and he saw it was nearly the evening. So when he runs back to society, the city was full of strange soldiers. And he says, "What's going on here? Where is Jeremiah and all the others?" And an old man said, "That was 66 years ago." It's a time travel story written in forbidden Biblical text. So is this a possible tale of time travel? *You decide!*

The Book of Baruch: *(One of the missing/forbidden books of the Christian Bible)*

- 5.22

For how much time has passed since my father Jeremiah sent me to the estate of Agrippa to bring a few figs, so that I might give them to the sick among the people?

- 5.23

And I went and got them, and when I came to a certain tree in the burning heat, I sat to rest a little; and I leaned my head on the basket and fell asleep.

- 5.24

And when I awoke I uncovered the basket of figs, supposing that I was late; and I found the figs dripping milk, just as I had collected them.

- 5.25

But you claim that the people have been taken captive into Babylon.

- 5.26

But that you might know, take the figs and see!

- 5.27

And he uncovered the basket of figs for the old man, and he saw them dripping milk.

- 5.28

And when the old man saw them, he said: "O my son, you are a righteous man, and God did not want you to see the desolation of the city, so he brought this trance upon you.

- 5.29

For behold it is 66 years today since the people were taken captive into Babylon.

- 5.30

But that you might learn, my son, that what I tell you is true -- look into the field and see that the ripening of the crops has not appeared.

- 5.31

And notice that the figs are not in season, and be enlightened."

- 5.32

Then Abimelech cried out in a loud voice, saying: I bless you, God of heaven and earth, the Rest of the souls of the righteous in every place!

- 5.33

Then he said to the old man: What month is this?

- 5.34

And he said: Nisan (which is Abib).

- 5.35

And taking some of the figs, he gave them to the old man and said to him: may God illumine your way to the city above, Jerusalem.

Time travel – India

in the ancient Indian text of the Mahabharata, written in the eighth century BC, King Raivata is described as traveling to the heavens to meet with the creator god – Brahma, only to return to Earth hundreds of years in the future. Some researchers believe this Hindu tale may be one of the oldest records of successful time travel in the ancient past. So there's in fact the story of a king called Raivata, and he is taken into space to see the gods, when he returns to the Earth he finds that many years have passed and in fact its been hundreds of years. Time travel? Some attribute that this is the kind of thing that would happen to space travelers and in time travel.

Urashima Tarō – Time travel

In Japan, the legend of Urashima Taro describes the tale of a fisherman's visit to the protector god of the sea – Ryūjin in an underwater palace for what seemed like only three days. When he returns to his fishing village, he finds that it's been 300 years that he's been gone. Everything that he knew of was long gone, his family, friends and his way of life, everything had changed in what seem to be for him only a few days.

One day a young fisherman named Urashima Tarō is fishing when he notices a group of children torturing a small turtle. Tarō saves it and lets it to go back to the sea. The next day, a huge turtle approaches him and tells him that the small turtle he had saved is the daughter of the Emperor of the Sea, Ryūjin, who wants to see him to thank him.

The turtle magically gives Tarō gills and brings him to the bottom of the sea, to the Palace of the Dragon God. There he meets the Emperor and the small turtle, who was now a lovely princess, Otohime.

Tarō stays there with her for a few days, but soon wants to go back to his village and see his aging mother, so he requests Otohime's permission to leave. The princess says she is sorry to see him go, but wishes him well and gives him a mysterious box called "tamatebako" which will protect him from harm but which she tells him never to open. Tarō grabs the box, jumps on the back of the same turtle that had brought him there, and soon is at the seashore.

He asks if anybody knows a man called Urashima Tarō. They answer that they had heard someone of that name had vanished at sea long ago. He discovers that 300 years have passed since the day he left for the bottom of the sea. Struck by grief, he absent-mindedly opens the box the princess had given him, from which bursts forth a cloud of white smoke. He is suddenly aged, his beard long and white, and his back bent. From the sea comes the sad, sweet voice of the princess: "I told you not to open that box. In it was your old age . . ."

▼

Some places across the globe, for years, have baffled the scientific community and historians alike. These places are mysterious and possess characteristics that have not been explained scientifically, even after decades or perhaps centuries of study and research that have gone into them. Radio frequency failure, compass malfunction, aircraft going off the radar and other unexplained malfunctions of navigational and electronic equipment are some of the bizarre events witnessed at these places over the years. Names such as Zona Di Silencio or the Zone of Silence, in Northern Mexico, The Bermuda Triangle, The Devils Triangle – off the Japanese coast, The Carnac Stones in France, The Gate of the Gods are predominant names in this enlistment. Here we try to find a few answers to some of these perplexities that have intrigued mankind over the years.

Perhaps the most famous (or rather infamous) of all the mysterious places is the **Bermuda Triangle**. For centuries this stretch of ocean covering more than 500,000 sq. miles located between Miami, Puerto Rico and Bermuda have tested the intelligences of scientists, experienced sailors and military investigators alike. Philip Coppens observes, *"we witness planes disappearing, weird lights being seen and a whole bunch of other weirdness in this tight corner of the Atlantic. Crews of ships have just disappeared without any sign of struggle and absolutely no trace of them have been found over the years"*. What caused the ships to disappear, why have the aeronautical and navigational equipment stopped working or changed course by itself?

Historical navigational records show, the anomalies of Bermuda Triangle is much older than most people realize. In fact it all started with Christopher Columbus' navigational log. He being such a respected sailor and an esoteric navigator, his logs about the journey to the new world is considered remarkably accurate. As he approached the area called the Bermuda Triangle, he witnessed strange phenomena such as compass malfunctions, the following night he witnessed a strange ball of fire hit the ocean. Also he witnessed weather abnormalities and a series of other events that cannot be explained as logically foreseen. So clearly, the events at Bermuda Triangle is not an urban myth that started in the threshold of the 20th century, its as old as there are accounts of people going into that area.

About 450 years after Columbus on December 5, 1945 the USAF faced the Bermuda Triangle's most perplexing mystery:

at 14:00 HRS., 5 torpedo bombers flew from an airbase at Fort Lauderdale, Florida on a routine training exercise. Not long into the 2 hour long mission, all 5 planes were suddenly gone. The Mystery was compounded when USAF sent a rescue mission and it too disappeared. 6 planes, all flown by skilled pilots, had flown into oblivion.

This incident sent shock waves across the United States Air Force and other defense establishments, because this was modern era, we had equipment's to trace them, we had radio, we had the RADAR and yet 6 planes had vanished without a trace. According to Philip Coppens, *"As if all of these aircraft have been snapped out of our reality, into 'something else' and of course what that something else is, that's the mystery of the Bermuda Triangle"*.

Over the years only a few have lived to tell us what anomalies occur at the Bermuda Triangle. However, American pilot Bruce Gernon is an exception. In 1970, Gernon, his father and a business associate were flying from the Bahamas to Florida, when Gernon reported seeing a strange cloud directly in front of their plane. Then as they approached, Gernon reported seeing the cloud form a doughnut shaped hole or a vortex. *"The hole was initially large but gradually narrowed down, and as I entered the 'tunnel', a strange thing happened. It was like looking down into a rifle barrel. It started swirling slowly counter clockwise, and I witnessed some intense electricity and there were flashes going on, and off and all I could see was a grayish/ yellowish fog, I call it electronic fog. I noticed that my instruments were malfunctioning, and at the same time I witnessed this unbelievable sensation."* Gernon says when he finally exited the tunnel he radioed the Miami ATC, but they could not see his plane on their Radar screen. *"And then about three minutes later the radio operator came online and he said he located me over Miami, and I couldn't believe it because I had been flying only for over 33 minutes, whereas the distance should have been about an hour and 33 minutes".* Could such a discrepancy in time and distance happen, and could ET's be using such gateways to travel to earth?

An interesting question!

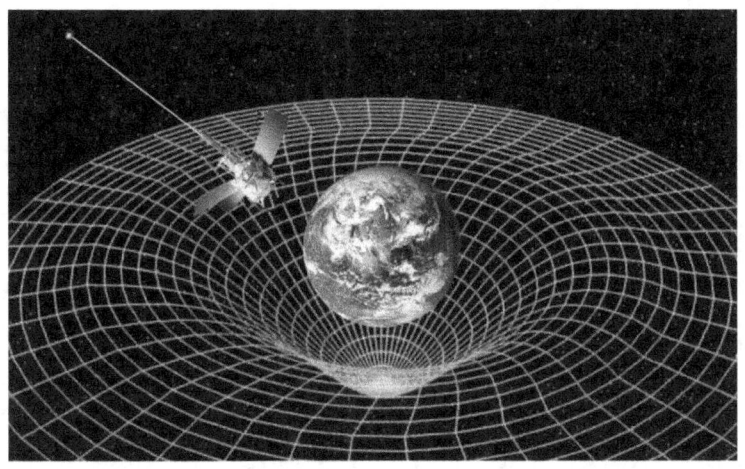

Herein comes the scientific angle. According to Albert Einstein's General Theory of Relativity, it is possible. Einstein's theory of being able to bend space using a gravitational pull, could be applied by the Alien crafts, by using these places to acquire and harness those extra amounts of energy, warp the distances – and thus attain a burst of speed in a direction of where they want to go. According to another thought process, *"Whenever there is an energy emission from a higher dimension or a higher plane, the energy emission would be in form of Vortices, so Vortices and Gateways are the same thing"*. Since wormholes are theoretically located all across the universe, could similar gateways be used for traveling across the universe?

Also could these gateways exist in smaller areas on Earth, and strange electromagnetic levels be the key to discovering them? In most of such reports we find a strange consistency involving strange electromagnetic phenomenon in form of strange vapor or cloud. According to David Childress, *"It's quite possible that Bermuda Triangle is one such inter-dimensional doorway that's used by these Aliens"*. With reports of UFOs appearing and ships and portals disappearing, some believe that Bermuda Triangle is a portal that works in both directions. So if, as Ancient Alien theorists believe, that this portal has been used by ET's to visit earth since antiquity, might we one day use the same portal to visit them? Also if there is a portal in the open waters of Bermuda, might there be more such portals on Land?

However, with the recent discovery of a crystal, partially translucent pyramid in the Bermuda Triangle – what we postulated may be about to change.

▼

Pyramid discovery challenges all archaeological theories:

A gigantic structure, perhaps larger than the Great Pyramid of Cheops in Egypt, and initially identified by a doctor in the 1960s, has been independently verified by diving teams from France and the U.S.

The discovery has rocked scientists around the world. Will they rush to investigate it? *No.* They're more likely to studiously ignore it. If pressed, they'll officially position themselves as highly skeptical—especially in light of the potential ramifications.

The pyramid could confirm some engineers' contentions that pyramids were originally created as massive power sources, support the claim that the ancient city-state of Atlantis did exist, or even provide answers to the mysterious goings-on that have been recorded since the 19th Century in the region of the Atlantic dubbed the *Bermuda Triangle*.

First discovered in 1968:

According to the history, the pyramid was accidentally discovered during 1968 by a doctor of naturopathy, Ray Brown of Mesa, Arizona.

Brown was in the Caribbean on vacation and making dives with friends in a region off the Bahamas known as "the Tongue of the Ocean." The area acquired that name because a tongue-shaped portion of the seabed extends out from the island before sharply dropping off into much greater depths.

When relating his discovery, the doctor explained he became separated from his diving friends underwater. While attempting to rejoin them, he came upon a massive structure rising from the ocean floor: a black, hulking object silhouetted against the lighter sun-filtered water. The object was shaped like a pyramid.

Because he was low on air, he didn't spend much time investigating the pyramid, but did find a strange crystal sphere.

He brought it to the surface with him, and later when the ancient crystal was studied researchers were astonished by its properties.

Is the crystal pyramid causing Triangle phenomena?

Some Triangle researchers have theorized for years that a strange energy source exists at the bottom of the sea within the region of the ocean affecting planes, ships, and boats.

A few investigators postulate that if the fabled Atlantis really did exist the remains of its mythical energy-vortex machine might still be intact at the bottom of the ocean. Such a machine, they claim, would likely be pyramidal-shaped and the original historical template that succeeding cultures around the globe copied much later.

Mysterious pyramids scattered across the world:

Pyramid structures have been discovered across North, Central, and South America; Eastern Europe; the icy tundra of Siberia; Northern and Central China; Alaska, and possibly Antarctica. The South Pole pyramid cannot be confirmed as it's deep under more than a mile of ice and images of it are controversial.

Years ago, mysterious ruins—the vestiges of an unknown culture—were discovered on a small island called Malden in the middle of the Pacific Ocean. The ruins were claimed to also have the remains of an ancient pyramid.

Believers in the ancient land of Lemuria (also called Mu) proposed that the ruins might be all that were left of that ancient land, while others speculated it might have been an outpost colony of Atlantis.

An anthropologist from the Bishop Museum in Honolulu, Hawaii explored the ruins back in 1924 and found no pyramid. What scientist Kenneth Emory did find, however, was evidence that a small Polynesian tribe once settled there briefly, perhaps no further back in time than the 16th Century.

Despite that finding, more revelations were to come from the tiny island during the ensuing years.

Researcher Mitch Williamson dug deeper into the mysteries.

Reporting on some of Williamson's amazing findings, Rich Hoffman, explorer and investigator, writes: "There are 40 stone temples on Malden Island that are described as similar in design to the buildings of Nan Madol on Pohnpei, some 3,400 miles (5,475 km) away. In fact, there is a basalt road that runs along the bottom of the Pacific Ocean which connects these islands under hundreds of feet of water.

This suggests a culture that is more than 50,000 years old and that this entire land mass was once above water supporting a civilization that had no trouble moving around tremendous stones to build very large, complicated societies which we know absolutely nothing about, other than the fact that someone built them and they are older than biblical history.

Yet, nobody discusses them because they don't fit into our understanding of the human race and their origins. Scientists have their diffusion theories of how migrants arrived in

North America using the land bridge of the Bering Straight and they are sticking with it.

The same can be said of the scattered ruins of the Caribbean that suggest a very large civilization extending from the coastal waters off the Florida Keys, toward the Bahamian waters, crossing near Bimini, and east into the Atlantic.

Cuba too has underwater ruins off its coast that may have been part of the same city-state complex."

Hoffman also mentions, almost in passing, the incredible report of explorer Tony Benik who made the momentous discovery of yet another huge pyramid under 10,000 feet of water in the middle of the Atlantic.

The pyramid, Benik claims, is capped with a huge crystal.

And if that's not enough, Hoffman shares the discovery of the Ari Marshall expedition in 1977. The team discovered a smaller pyramid off Cay Sal in the Bahamas. Marshall snapped underwater photos of the pyramid that's submerged beneath 150 feet of water.

According to Marshall's account the mystery pyramid glows. He also reported the water around the pyramid was luminescent and glistening white water flowed out of openings in the pyramid.

Despite the water at that depth being dark (not much light reaches that far down), the water surrounding the amazing pyramid was lit by the glow from the structure and appeared like a phosphorescent green color.

No follow-up exploration has ever been done of the find.

Is it possible that the Ice Age flood destroyed Atlantis?

Did Atlantis really exist? Is Plato's description the only history left of the—perhaps—mythical land?

For an answer, Hoffman turns to the story of the amateur archaeologist who discovered the legendary city of Troy, Heinrich Schliemann: "The man who found and excavated the famous ruins of Troy (which historians thought was only a legend), reportedly left a written account of his discovery of a vase with a metal unknown to scientists who examined it, in the famous Priam Treasure. Inside it are glyphs in Phoenician stating that it was from King Chronos of Atlantis. Identical pottery was found in Tiajuanaco, Bolivia."

If Atlantis did exist, it probably existed during the end of the last Ice Age. The story of its sinking relates to the massive floods and rising ocean when the oversized Arctic icecap suddenly receded with catastrophic results for much of the Northern Hemisphere.

At the end of the last Ice Age sea levels were nearly 400 feet lower than present day levels. Once the waters began to rise, they rose swiftly. Conceivably, no technology then, or now, could have saved Atlantis from its watery grave.

Properties of crystal pyramids:

Some theories of Atlantis propose the island city's power pyramids were made of crystal, or their tops were capped with a crystalline substance.

Could such a thing actually generate, store, and distribute energy on demand?

Yes.

Experimenters discovered decades ago that pyramids do tend to act in some ways like a natural electrical capacitor gathering and storing energy around them. The larger the pyramid, the greater the capacity of gathering and storing energy. A pyramid's composition is important too. Having one made of crystal, or an apex made of crystal, could vastly increase its power.

Crystal has long been known to have energy applications and exhibits natural piezoelectrical properties.

Early radio used germanium crystals to capture the radio waves and convert them into electrical signals that could be processed and broadcast through headphones into sound waves duplicating the human voice, music, and other sounds.

Pyramid power, say investigators, is intrinsic to the pyramid shape. It's an architecture that's proven to function as an energy accumulator and amplifier of energetic force.

As if to prove the investigators' assertions true, recently some of the world's pyramids began discharging beams of raw energy into space. *Why?*

Ponder this:

The bottom line? Pyramids are intrinsically *unnatural*, natural generators of power. Who created them, and why? – They didn't just grow out of the ground they occupy! But do we really want to know? Whether or not we want to know – we NEED to know. Understanding them may be the only way we can save ourselves; because, if they were created to supply the atmosphere with an energy grid that keeps our souls from leaving this place (eternally enslaving mankind), keeping us from returning to the source (the One True God of All Creation) – until He returns – perhaps we need to destroy them! Is this just one of the 'many things' that Jesus came to save us from? Mind-blowing concept, is it not?!

Pyramids and the

'Cavity Structural Effect'

Barry Carter calls attention to another property that pyramids exhibit called the "Cavity Structural Effect" (CSE) by its discoverer, Dr. Viktor S. Grebennikov. The scientist employed the CSE to construct a rudimentary anti-gravity platform.

Carter explains that "Grebennikov also claimed that he could feel energies emitting from the apex of a pyramid: 'You will soon pick up an active zone, a "clot", where the Egyptians had their tombs. Another active zone (a "flame") above the top of the pyramid is also well-perceived by the indicator if you drag its end over the top. The "clot" and the "flame" are well-felt by the finger inserted into the pyramid, or your palm moved above it after some practice. The pyramid effect, which generated many scary and mysterious stories over the centuries, is one of the CSE manifestations.'"

Another deadly phenomenon that pyramids may create:

Energy Vortexcs

Besides the time and spatial anomalies reported in the Triangle, some survivors of terrifying incidents there have reported huge, swirling vortices suddenly appearing and disappearing .

Evidence exists that some missing ships may have gone missing because of this phenomenon.

Observations of some of the submerged pyramids reveals they sporadically generate intense vortices in the ocean water flowing around them. Those vortices may be caused by a discharge of internal energy.

If those submerged, pyramids also discharge massive energy through their apexes that could account for the formation of deadly vortices on the surface of the sea that swallows up whole ships along with their doomed crews.

Future expeditions to these mysterious pyramids may finally uncover the truth and reveal amazing ancient technology.

Unfortunately, deep-sea archaeology is very expensive, and not well funded. Most dives are to ancient wrecks that promise riches to risk-taking treasure hunters.

And, of course, the world's universities are not especially eager to explore the idea that very ancient ruins containing high technology may exist that challenges virtually all of the foundations of their pet theories.

◊◊◊

A little over 400 miles south of El Paso Texas, in northern Mexico, stretches a remote and rugged section of high desert. This area near the town of Ceballos is referred to by the locals as *Zona Del Silencio* or the Zone of Silence. Its at the epicenter of some of the strangest phenomena ever recorded on earth. Nothing seems to work in this area, the cellphone drops out of range, the radio doesn't catch any signal, the compass just keeps spinning, its completely bizarre. There are strange rocks everywhere, we even witness strange mutated animals in the area.

The Zone of Silence was first identified by Francisco Sarabia, a Mexican pilot who claimed that his radio mysteriously failed to function while flying over the area. Its located between the same parallel as the Bermuda Triangle i.e. between 26°N and 28°N of equator and as a result goes and connects to the Egyptian Pyramids.

On July 11, 1970 when the USAF lost an Athena Missile that was launched from its facility at Green River, Utah. It was programed to land 700 miles away at the White Sands Missile Range, New Mexico. But due to some unexplained reason, the missile flew several hundred miles past its range to the Zone of Silence. According to a NASA

Spokesperson, the missile mysteriously got pulled into the Zone of Silence. But this is not the only thing that got 'pulled' into this area.

Ancient Alien Theorists believe that an unusually large number of meteorites have crashed into the area. According to Logan Hawkes – the author of The Mexico less Traveled, *"there is a very strong magnetic signature to this place and this has been proven scientifically, however we need more research to establish, whether this magnetism is strong enough to pull space debris like meteorites. And I don't think such research is happening right now"*.

Starting 3000 years ago, the Anasazi Indians inhabited the area to the North of Zona Del Silencio, today's American Southwest. The word Anasazi means Ancient Ones, and they paid great attention to the stars. Scientists have established that at about 1054 AD, a supernova explosion was visible from earth. Many believe that that first ever drawing of this event was found inside an Anasazi cave dwelling. South of the Zone of Silence, established cultures like the Maya, seem to have exact knowledge of such celestial events. Its often debated that Anasazi and the Mesoamerican cultures often used the Zone of Silence as their meeting place. But what other connections exist between these cultures and are they of celestial origin?

Both the Anasazi and the Mesoamericans were great believers in Sky People – of beings who came from the sky. And the description of these heavenly people is consistent in their reports, as tall, pale skinned, white haired beings, and that is not indigenous to the region, but does match the South American descriptions of their Gods.

According to the local legends, these ancient Gods made themselves known to the ancient people, is possible that these heavenly people are still letting themselves be known: Contactors – and Contactees?

We have established reports of UFO sightings in the region and its considerably higher than any other area in the vicinity. One of the most prominent ones came from the town of Ceballos one summer afternoon, when hundreds of people reported an object hovering over the desert on the outskirts of the town. It was described to be about 100 meters wide and had multicolored lights flashing, it wasn't doing anything, but was just hovering over the desert. After a while it just 'took off' and headed towards the Zone of Silence.

According to the Ancient Alien Theorists, there is a connection between the magnetic signature of this place, the alien Gods and the present day UFO sightings, however are there more such places across the world that could provide us more direct evidences of such occurrences in the past?

Located about 800 miles South East of Lima, Peru on the shores of Lake Titicaca is a sight that have mystified visitors from all around the world. Shamans still come and offer prayers at a rock wall on this high plateau as they have done for generations. This is called **Puerta del Hijo Marka** – or the Gate of the Gods. Its a doorway carved into solid rock. According to David Childress," it really appears to be a Gateway, but it doesn't really go anywhere". It's literally in the middle of nowhere, at 14,000 ft., yet this is a perfect rectangle carved out of a solid block of rock and right at the bottom it's got another indent in it, that looks like a door. The Peruvians refer to it as the Gate of the Gods.

But the baffling question is, why would someone make a doorway, in the middle of nowhere at 14000 ft. and one that doesn't go anywhere? There has to be a way to get across this. According to Inca legend, the first priest Amaro Muro is said to have traveled through this doorway, using a special object to activate it turning the solid rock into what is known as the Star Gate. This Star Gate was activated by help of a golden disc and this golden disc fell from the sky. He held the golden disc into the gateway in a recessed area, and the gateway activated and he passed though it, never to be seen again.

Archeologists have noticed a depression at the center of the doorway, and it is believed it was perhaps this depression, where the golden disc was placed. This disc was made of gold and other precious metals, and perhaps was a technological device which had the ability to open up inter-dimensional gateways. Furthermore, according to the local legends, these priests were called space brothers and came from other worlds. May they have come to earth through this Gateway? However, could a device to activate this door actually exist? And if so, where would the doorway lead? The Gate of the Gods could well be one end of a wormhole, a type of portal used to connect to another part of the universe or another dimension.

Wormholes are an accepted element of Theoretical and Particle Physics. But have they actually existed on some of our world's most mysterious places. The aliens are perhaps coming to earth in inter dimensional crafts that allow then to travel through hyper space. And they can travel between their dimension and ours in literally no time. But to do that they have to travel through these wormholes and enter planet earth through a portal. What if one end of the portal does really exist at Puerta del Hijo Marka? Does it qualify for a reason why Peru has always been considered as a focal point of UFO and ET activities?

Lake Titicaca has all sorts of strange lights associated with it. All the more, people have reported seeing strange blue balls of fire and even alien crafts coming out of the lake, and even reported seeing beings in some of the sightings. And these beings are reported to have been tall, pale skinned and white haired, completely non indigenous to the local population.

Another way the Ancient Aliens might have traveled is through Teleportation. But is it possible to make an object disappear at one place and make it appear in another? At the Max Planck Institute, they have already been able to dematerialize sub atomic particles, and made them reappear somewhere else. This could be a secret the ancient people knew. The area around Puerta del Hijo Marka still holds the energy and its evident as you approach the area.

But is Puerta del Hijo Marka the only mysterious place in Peru? Are there other mysterious places here? High up in the mountains of Peru, 850 miles from the Gate of the Gods, is a breathtaking 2 mile long plateau another area of reportedly high energy. For centuries it has been a powerful scared place among the Incan people. Its called **Markawasi**. Markawasi is said to have very bizarre energy patterns. According to Kathy Moore, "Markawasi is a place of wizards and genies and people treat it with a great deal of veneration. When people go there, they experience a special kind of energy – or a state of Euphoria". Most geologists believe that the stone figures at Markawasi are naturally formed through weathering and other natural processes. But is there more here than first meets the eye?

Some consider Markawasi as a massive sculpture garden left behind by some ancient civilization. Could this then be not just a collection of rocks, but a sanctuary of stone monuments made by ancient civilization hundreds of thousands of years ago. Researcher Daniel Rousseau was the first to make this claim in 1952. According to Kathy

Moore, "He was shown a photograph of a colossal head made of stone, up in the high mountains above Lima. He made an expedition just to see the stone face, and one at Markawasi, he was astonished to see there were hundreds of such carved stones". Among these figures people have been able to decipher few very prominent ones – seen on the next page:

▼

African Queen

Taweret

181

Frogs

Camel

182

If these figures are man made, who may have carved them? The local legend says that its a place of ancient giant gods. In fact when the Spanish chroniclers came to Peru and investigated the shamanic traditions there, they were told about a god named Viracocha who came in garb of man to inspect his territory, and he had given men different orders, and there were some who disobeyed them, and he promptly turned them to stone.

The name Markawasi provides a clue to the time and origin of the place. The name itself predates the Incan Empire. According to Daniel Rousseau, the name Markawasi probably meant two storied house and referred to the strange complex of buildings located on the site. Rousseau further states that the ancient people who built Markawasi were called the Masma and supposedly, Peru was not their only home. Robert M Schoch observes, *"The Masma were very ancient, very advanced civilization, who seemed to have had a global existence and have traveled worldwide at a very early period, in prerecorded history.*

Rousseau spent a lot of time looking for evidences of this civilization and seemed to have finally found it in Markawasi. He thought Markawasi was some kind of a sculpture garden built by the Masma". If a global community of such advancement existed, whet happened to it? Was it, as some believe wiped out in the great flood, described in the Bible? Was this created as a record of events or a memento that could be passed on to future generations, because they thought they were not going to live forever and they wanted to leave some kind of a record or warning for future generations.

The next perplexing question is, if such an advanced civilization existed in antiquity, where did they come from. According to Author, George Hunt Williamson, *"Markawasi was a sacred forest where the Ancient Aliens met to plan for the future, and many UFO researchers believe they are still returning to this day"*.

David Childress says, *"the most famous UFO photograph from Peru, was taken by a businessman near Markawasi, who himself was trekking up to the Markawasi Plateau, and when he saw down the valley he saw a bright silvery disk floating in the valley in broad daylight. This happened in the 70s"*.

Does Markawasi emit a special kind of energy and if so, have they been attracting visitors for thousands of years. Although we do not clearly

184

understand the anomalies in these areas, however the presence of a high energy emissions, electromagnetic impulses, geomagnetic anomalies, subterranean electricity and such possibilities cannot be undermined or overruled.

Is there a reason why these inter dimensional portals appear on certain spots on our planet? Is there a pattern that could be formed. Is there a code and if yes, did our ancestors know about it? According to the ancient Astronaut theorists, the energy fields around the world are not randomly located. they are connected by what is known as the **World Energy Grid** – a geometric pattern of energy that crisscrosses the globe.

According to David Childress, *"the energy fields across the world are stronger in some areas as compared to the others, and in these areas they form sort of a Vortex, thereby making the energy more useful in its sense"*.

The Earth Grid Theory States that the Earth Energy Fields are connected with one another by means of a geometric pattern, and this has existed since time earth was created.

The concept of Energy Grid, for our civilization extends back to the Pythagorean

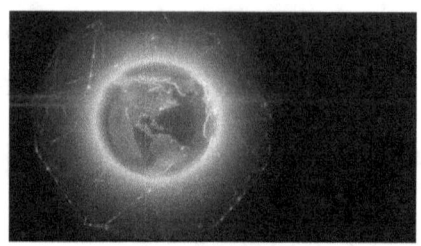

School of Thought in ancient Greece. The theory states that the Earth is a dodecahedron (δωδεκάεδρον) and the geometric shapes and forms is all that matter is composed of, including the Earth. Hence it draws a parallel between them causing an energy interchange at certain prominent points of the dodecahedron.

Another puzzling phenomena brought to notice by French UFO Investigator Mitchel, was that the UFO sightings do not happen in random. There is a route map and a pattern to where the UFO sightings happen, and it follows not only the exact longitude patterns, but also the Earth Energy Grid.

Mitchel's report was based upon every single UFO sighting since the Roswell incident. Scientists now believe that the concentration of energy levels and UFO sightings are not a matter of coincidence. The megalithic structures in these special locations were crested to amplify the energy fields. Its a Theory known as **Geomancy**.

By creating pyramid shaped structures and tall stone obelisks, we can magnify and channelize this power. It works on earth exactly the same way acupuncture works on the human body.

In Europe, thousands of km of land stretches have been logically connected through straight lines, they are called Ley Lines. These ley lines stretch all the way from England, to France down to Italy. And on these ley lines we have names of places, and the common factor to all of these names is the word 'star'. This cannot be attributed to the stone age man. Someone told them to do so. And they most often were called Gods, or people who came from the skies. So the question is were these people extraterrestrials?

Unless the scientific community is logically able to derive answers to some of the most mysterious places on earth, we will only be left with lingering questions, and ones that cannot be answered with the approach the conventional scholarship have been taking since time immemorial. Are some of these places really inter dimensional portals, did the ancient aliens transport them through these

Star Gates to another dimension. What we are left with is a litany of perplexing questions that need answers. And answers will come, but only if we **THINK** – *and put aside easy explanations!*

The truth is seldom EASY!

Classic Chills

190

Pale Man

(Phantoms walk these halls!)

by

Julius Long

*It absolutely kills me – that I can't find a
picture of this wonderful author!*

Julius W. Long

(Ohio Lawyer & Author)

Rest in Peace

- **Legal Name:** Long, Julius W.
- **Birthdate:** 1907
- **Death date:** 1955

Other works by him:

- *Death's Dancing Master (1937)*
- *He Walked by Day (1934)*
- *Merely Murder (1944)*
- *Nightcap of Terror (1937)*
- *Possession (1934)*

- *Supper for Thirteen (**1934**)*
- *The Dead Man's Story (**1933**)*
- *The Defense Rests (1938)*
- *The Execution of Lucarno (**1937**)*
- *The Late Mourner (**1934**)*
- *The Pale Man (**1934**)*
- *The Vaunsburg Plague (**1937**)*

(Or dimensional rift?)

A queer little tale, about the eccentric behavior of a strange guest in a country hotel.

I have not yet met the man in No. 212. I do not even know his name. He never patronizes the hotel restaurant, and he does not use the lobby. On the three occasions when we passed each other by, we did not speak, although we nodded in a semi-cordial, noncommittal way. I should like very much to make his acquaintance. It is lonesome in this dreary place. With the exception of the aged lady down the corridor, the only permanent guests are the man in No. 212 and myself. However, I

195

should not complain, for this utter quiet is precisely what the doctor prescribed.

I wonder if the man in No. 212, too, has come here for a rest. He is so very pale. Yet I can not believe that he is ill, for his paleness is not of a sickly cast, but rather wholesome in its ivory clarity. His carriage is that of a man enjoying the best of health. He is tall and straight. He walks erectly and with a brisk, athletic stride. His pallor is no doubt congenital, else he would quickly tan under this burning, summer sun.

He must have traveled here by auto, for he certainly was not a passenger on the train that brought me, and he checked in only a short time after my arrival. I had briefly rested in my room and was walking down the stairs when I encountered him ascending with his bag. It is odd that our venerable bell-boy did not show him to his room.

It is odd, too, that, with so many vacant rooms in the hotel, he should have chosen No. 212 at the extreme rear. The building is a long, narrow affair three stories high. The rooms are all on the east side, as the west wall is flush with a decrepit business building. The corridor is long and drab, and its stiff, bloated paper exudes a musty, unpleasant odor. The feeble electric bulbs that light it shine dimly as from a tomb. Revolted by this corridor, I insisted vigorously upon being given No. 201, which is at the front and blessed with southern exposure. The room clerk, a disagreeable fellow with a Hitler mustache, was very reluctant to let me have it, as it is ordinarily reserved for his more profitable transient trade. I fear my stubborn insistence has made him an enemy.

If only I had been as self-assertive thirty years ago! I should now be a full-fledged professor instead of a broken-down assistant. I still smart from the cavalier manner in which the president of the university summarily recommended my vacation. No doubt he acted for my best interests. The people who have dominated my poor life invariably have.

Oh, well, the summer's rest will probably do me considerable good. It is pleasant to be away from the university. There is something positively gratifying about the absence of the graduate student face.

If only it were not so lonely! I must devise a way of meeting the pale man in No. 212. Perhaps the room clerk can arrange matters.

I HAVE been here exactly a week, and if there

is a friendly soul in this miserable little town, he has escaped my notice. Although the tradespeople accept my money with flattering eagerness, they studiously avoid even the most casual conversation. I am afraid I can never cultivate their society unless I can arrange to have my ancestors recognized as local residents for the last hundred and fifty years.

Despite the coolness of my reception, I have been frequently venturing abroad. In the back of my mind I have cherished hopes that I might encounter the pale man in No. 211. Incidentally, I wonder why he has moved from No. 212. There is certainly little advantage in coming only one room nearer to the front. I noticed the change yesterday when I saw him coming out of his new room.

We nodded again, and this time I thought I detected a certain malign satisfaction in his somber, black eyes. He must know that I am eager to make his acquaintance, yet his manner forbids overtures. If he wants to make me go all the way, he can go to the devil. I am not the sort to run after anybody. Indeed, the surly diffidence of the room clerk has been enough to prevent me from questioning him about his mysterious guest. I WONDER where the pale man takes his meals. I have been absenting myself from the

198

hotel restaurant and patronizing the restaurants outside. At each I have ventured inquiries about the man in No. 210. No one at any restaurant remembered his having been there. Perhaps he has entrée into the Brahmin homes of this town. And again, he may have found a boarding-house. I shall have to learn if there be one.

The pale man must be difficult to please, for he has again changed his room. I am baffled by his conduct. If he is so desirous of locating himself more conveniently in the hotel, why does he not move to No. 202, which is the nearest available room to the front?

Perhaps I can make his inability to locate himself permanently an excuse for starting a conversation. "I see we are closer neighbors now," I might casually say. But that is too banal. I must await a better opportunity.

He has done it again! He is now occupying No. 209. I am intrigued by his little game. I waste hours trying to fathom its point. What possible motive could he have? I should think he would get on the hotel people's nerves. I wonder what our combination bellhop-chambermaid thinks of having to prepare four rooms for a single guest. If he were not stone-deaf, I would ask him. At present I feel too exhausted to attempt such an enervating conversation.

I am tremendously interested in the pale man's next move. He must either skip a room or remain where he is, for a permanent guest, a very old lady, occupies No. 208. She has not budged-from her room since I have been here, and I imagine that she does not intend to.

I wonder what the pale man will do. I await his decision with the nervous excitement of a devotee of the track on the eve of a big race. After all, I have so little diversion.

Well, the mysterious guest was not forced to remain where he was, nor did he have to skip a room. The lady in No. 208 simplified matters by conveniently dying. No one knows the cause of her death, but it is generally attributed to old age. She was buried this morning. I was among the curious few who attended her funeral. When I returned home from the mortuary, I was in time to see the pale man leaving her room. Already he has moved in.

He favored me with a smile whose meaning I have tried in vain to decipher. I can not but believe that he meant it to have some

significance. He acted as if there were between us some secret that I failed to appreciate. But, then, perhaps his smile was meaningless after all and only ambiguous by chance, like that of the Mona Lisa.

My man of mystery now resides in No. 207, and I am not the least surprised. I would have been astonished if he had not made his scheduled move, I have almost given up trying to understand his eccentric conduct. I do not know a single thing more about him than I knew the day he arrived. I wonder whence he came. There is something indefinably foreign about his manner. I am curious to hear his voice. I like to imagine that he speaks the exotic tongue of some far-away country. If only I could somehow inveigle him into conversation! I wish that I were possessed of the glib assurance of a college boy, who can address himself to the most distinguished celebrity without batting an eye. It is no wonder that I am only an assistant professor.

I am worried. This morning I awoke to find myself lying prone upon the floor. I was fully clothed. I must have fallen exhausted there after I returned to my room last night.

I wonder if my condition is more serious than I had suspected. Until now I have been inclined to discount the fears of those who have pulled a long face about me. For the first time I recall the prolonged hand-clasp of the president when he bade me good-bye from the university. Obviously he never expected to see me alive again.

Of course I am not that unwell. Nevertheless, I must be more careful. Thank heaven I have no dependents to worry about. I have not even a wife, for I was never willing to exchange the loneliness of a bachelor for the loneliness of a husband.

I can say in all sincerity that the prospect of death does not frighten me. Speculation about life beyond the grave has always bored me. Whatever it is, or is not, I'll try to get along.

I have been so preoccupied about the sudden turn of my own affairs that I have neglected to make note of a most extraordinary incident. The pale man has done an astounding thing. He has skipped three rooms and moved all the way to No. 203. We are now very close neighbors. We shall meet oftener, and my chances for making his acquaintance are now greater.

I have confined myself to my bed during the last few days and have had my food brought to me. I even called a local doctor, whom I suspect to be a quack. He looked me over with professional indifference and told me not to leave my room. For some reason he does not want me to climb stairs. For this bit of information he received a ten-dollar bill which, as I directed him, he fished out of my coat pocket. A pickpocket could not have done it better.

He had not been gone long when I was visited by the room clerk. That worthy suggested with a great show of kindly concern that I use the facilities of the local hospital. It was so modern and all that. With more firmness than I have been able to muster in a long time, I gave him to understand that I intended to remain where I am. Frowning sullenly, he stiffly retired. The doctor must have paused long enough downstairs to tell him a pretty story. It is obvious that he is afraid I shall die in his best room.

The pale man is up to his old tricks. Last night, when I tottered down the hall, the door of No. 202 was ajar. Without thinking, I looked inside. The pale man sat in a rocking-chair idly smoking a cigarette. He looked up into my eyes and smiled that peculiar, ambiguous smile that has so deeply puzzled me. I moved on down the corridor, not so much mystified as annoyed. The whole mystery of the man's conduct is beginning to irk me. It is all so inane, so utterly lacking in motive.

I feel that I shall never meet the pale man. But, at least, I am going to learn his identity. Tomorrow I shall ask for the room clerk and deliberately interrogate him.

I know now. I know the identity of the pale man, and I know the meaning of his smile.

Early this afternoon I summoned the room clerk to my bedside.

"Please tell me," I asked abruptly, "who is the man in No. 202?"

The clerk stared wearily and uncomprehendingly.

"You must be mistaken. That room is unoccupied."

"Oh, but it is," I snapped in irritation. "I myself saw the man there only two nights ago. He is a tall, handsome fellow with dark eyes and hair. He is unusually pale. He checked in the day that I arrived."

The hotel man regarded me dubiously, as if I were trying to impose upon him.

"But I assure you there is no such person in the house. As for his checking in when you did, you were the only guest we registered that day."

"What? Why, I've seen him twenty times! First he had No. 212 at the end of the corridor. Then he kept moving toward the front. Now he's next door in No. 202."

The room clerk threw up his hands.

"You're crazy!" he exclaimed, and I saw that he meant what he said.

I shut up at once and dismissed him. After he had gone, I heard him rattling the knob of the pale man's door. There is no doubt that he believes the room to be empty.

Thus it is that I can now understand the events of the past few weeks. I now comprehend the significance of the death in No. 207. I even feel partly responsible for the old lady's passing. After all, I brought the pale man with me. But it was not I who fixed his path. Why he chose to approach me room after room through the length of this dreary hotel, why his path crossed the threshold of the woman in No. 207, those mysteries I can not explain.

I suppose I should have guessed his identity when he skipped the three rooms the night I fell unconscious upon the floor. In a single night of triumph he advanced until he was almost to my door.

He will be coming by and by to inhabit this room, his ultimate goal. When he comes, I shall at least be able to return his smile of grim recognition.

Meanwhile, I have only to wait beyond my bolted door.

◇◇◇

The door swings slowly open....

The Striding-Place

by

Gertrude Atherton

GERTRUDE ATHERTON

Gertrude Franklin Horn Atherton (October 30, 1857 – June 14, 1948) was a prominent and prolific American author. Many of her novels are set in her home state, California. Her best-seller *Black Oxen* (1923) was made into a silent movie of the same name. In addition to novels, she wrote short stories, essays, and articles for magazines and newspapers on such issues as feminism, politics, and war. She was strong-willed, independent-minded, and sometimes controversial.

I, continental and detached, tired early of grouse shooting. To stand propped against a sod fence while his host's workmen routed up the birds with long poles and drove them towards the waiting guns, made him feel himself a parody on the ancestors who had roamed the moors and forests of this West Riding of Yorkshire in hot pursuit of game worth the killing. But when in England in August he always accepted whatever proffered for the season, and invited his host to shoot pheasants on his estates in the South. The amusements of life, he argued, should be accepted with the same philosophy as its ills.

It had been a bad day. A heavy rain had made the moor so spongy that it fairly sprang beneath the feet. Whether or not the grouse had haunts of their own, wherein they were immune from rheumatism, the bag had been small. The women, too, were an unusually dull lot, with the exception of a new-minded džbutante who bothered Weigall at dinner by demanding the verbal restoration of the vague paintings on the vaulted roof above them.

But it was no one of these things that sat on Weigall's mind as, when the other men went up to bed, he let himself out of the castle and sauntered down to the river. His intimate friend, the companion of his boyhood, the chum of his college days, his fellow-traveller in many lands, the man for whom he possessed stronger affection than for all men, had mysteriously disappeared two days ago, and his track might have sprung to the upper air for all trace he had left behind him. He had been a guest on the adjoining estate during the past week, shooting with the fervor of the true sportsman, making love in the intervals to Adeline Cavan, and apparently in the best of spirits. As far as was known there was nothing to lower his mental mercury, for his rent-roll was a large one, Miss Cavan blushed whenever he looked at her, and, being one of the best shots in England, he was never happier than in August. The suicide theory was preposterous, all agreed, and there was as little reason to believe him murdered. Nevertheless, he had walked out of March Abbey two nights ago without hat or overcoat, and had not been seen since.

The country was being patrolled night and day. A hundred keepers and workmen were beating the woods and poking the bogs on the moors, but as yet not so much as a handkerchief had been found.

Weigall did not believe for a moment that Wyatt Gifford was dead, and although it was impossible not to be affected by the general uneasiness, he was disposed to be more angry than frightened. At Cambridge Gifford had been an incorrigible practical joker, and by no means had outgrown the habit; it would be like him to cut across the country in his evening clothes, board a cattle-train, and amuse himself touching up the picture of the sensation in West Riding.

However, Weigall's affection for his friend was too deep to companion with tranquility in the present state of doubt, and, instead of going to bed early with the other men, he determined to walk until ready for sleep. He went down to

215

the river and followed the path through the woods. There was no moon, but the stars sprinkled their cold light upon the pretty belt of water flowing placidly past wood and ruin, between green masses of overhanging rocks or sloping banks tangled with tree and shrub, leaping occasionally over stones with the harsh notes of an angry scold, to recover its equanimity the moment the way was clear again.

It was very dark in the depths where Weigall trod. He smiled as he recalled a remark of Gifford's: "An English wood is like a good many other things in life-- very promising at a distance, but a hollow mockery when you get within. You see daylight on both sides, and the sun freckles the very bracken. Our woods need the night to make them seem what they ought to be--what they once were, before our ancestors' descendants demanded so much more money, in these so much more various days."

Weigall strolled along, smoking, and thinking of his friend, his pranks--many of which had done more credit to his imagination than this--and recalling conversations that had lasted the night through. Just before the end of the London season they had walked the streets one hot night after a party, discussing the various theories of the soul's destiny. That afternoon they had met at the coffin of a college friend whose mind had been a blank for the past three years. Some months previously they had called at the asylum to see him. His expression had been senile, his face imprinted with the record of debauchery. In death the face was placid, intelligent, without ignoble lineation--the face of the man they had known at college. Weigall and Gifford had no time to comment there, and the afternoon and evening were full; but, coming forth from the house of festivity together, they had reverted almost at once to the topic.

"I cherish the theory," Gifford had said, "that the soul sometimes lingers in the body after death. During madness, of course, it is an impotent prisoner, albeit a conscious one. Fancy its agony, and its horror! What more natural than that, when the life-spark goes out, the tortured soul should take possession of the vacant skull and triumph once more for a few hours while old friends look their last? It has had time to repent while compelled to crouch and behold the result of its work, and it has shrived itself into a state of comparative purity. If I had my way, I should stay inside my bones until the coffin had gone into its niche, that I might obviate for my poor old comrade the tragic impersonality of death. And I should like to see justice done to it, as it were--to see it lowered among its ancestors with the ceremony and solemnity that are its due. I am afraid that if I dissevered myself too quickly, I should yield to curiosity and hasten to investigate the mysteries of space."

"You believe in the soul as an independent entity, then--that it and the vital principle are not one and the same?"

"Absolutely. The body and soul are twins, life comrades--sometimes friends, sometimes enemies, but always loyal in the last instance. Some day, when I am tired of the world, I shall go to India and become a mahatma, solely for the pleasure of receiving proof during life of this independent relationship."

"Suppose you were not sealed up properly, and returned after one of your astral flights to find your earthly part unfit for habitation? It is an experiment I don't think I should care to try, unless even juggling with soul and flesh had palled."

"That would not be an uninteresting predicament. I should rather enjoy experimenting with broken machinery."

218

The high wild roar of water smote suddenly upon Weigall's ear and checked his memories. He left the wood and walked out on the huge slippery stones which nearly close the River Wharf at this point, and watched the waters boil down into the narrow pass with their furious untiring energy. The black quiet of the woods rose high on either side. The stars seemed colder and whiter just above. On either hand the perspective of the river might have run into a rayless cavern. There was no lonelier spot in England, nor one which had the right to claim so many ghosts, if ghosts there were.

Weigall was not a coward, but he recalled uncomfortably the tales of those that had been done to death in the Strid.1 Wordsworth's Boy of Egremond had been disposed of by the practical Whitaker; but countless others, more venturesome than wise, had gone down into that narrow boiling course, never to appear in the still pool a few yards beyond. Below the great rocks, which form the walls of the Stride, was believed to be a natural vault, on to whose shelves the dead were drawn. The spot had an ugly fascination. Weigall stood, visioning skeletons, unconfined and green, the home of the eyeless things that had devoured all that had covered and filled that rattling symbol of man's mortality; then fell to wondering if any one had attempted to leap the Stride of late. It was covered with slime; he had never seen it look so treacherous.

He shuddered and turned away, impelled, despite his manhood, to flee the spot. As he did so, something tossing in the foam below the fall--something as white, yet independent of it--caught his eye and arrested his step. Then he saw that it was describing a contrary motion to the rushing water--an upward backward motion. Weigall stood rigid, breathless; he fancied he heard the crackling of his hair. Was that a hand? It thrust itself still higher above the boiling foam, turned sidewise, and four frantic fingers were distinctly visible against the black rock beyond.

Weigall's superstitious terror left him. A man was there, struggling to free himself from the suction beneath the Stride, swept down, doubtless, but a moment before his arrival, perhaps as he stood with his back to the current.

He stepped as close to the edge as he dared. The hand doubled as if in imprecation, shaking savagely in the face of that force,

which leaves its creatures to immutable law; then spread wide again, clutching, expanding, crying for help as audibly as the human voice.

Weigall dashed to the nearest tree, dragged and twisted off a branch with his strong arms, and returned as swiftly to the Stride. The hand was in the same place, still gesticulating as wildly; the body was undoubtedly caught in the rocks below, perhaps already half-way along one of those hideous shelves. Weigall let himself down upon a lower rock, braced his shoulder against the mass beside him, then, leaning out over the water, thrust the branch into the hand. The fingers clutched it convulsively. Weigall tugged powerfully, his own feet dragged perilously near the edge. For a moment he produced no impression, then an arm shot above the waters.

The blood sprang to Weigall's head; he was choked with the impression that the Stride had him in her roaring hold, and he saw nothing. Then the mist cleared. The hand and arm were nearer, although the rest of the body was still concealed by the foam. Weigall peered out with distended eyes. The meager light revealed in the cuffs links of a peculiar device. The fingers clutching the branch were as familiar.

Weigall forgot the slippery stones, the terrible death if he stepped too far. He pulled with passionate will and muscle. Memories flung themselves into the hot light of his brain, trooping rapidly upon each other's heels, as in the thought of the drowning. Most of the pleasures of his life, good and bad, were identified in some way with this friend. Scenes of college days, of travel, where they had deliberately sought adventure and stood between one another and death upon more occasions than one, of hours of delightful companionship among the treasures of art, and others in the pursuit of pleasure, flashed like the changing particles of a kaleidoscope. Weigall had loved several women; but he

222

would have flouted in these moments the thought that he had ever loved any woman as he loved Wyatt Gifford. There were so many charming women in the world, and in the thirty-two years of his life he had never known another man to whom he had cared to give his intimate friendship.

He threw himself on his face. His wrists were cracking, the skin was torn from his hands. The fingers still gripped the stick. There was life in them yet.

Suddenly something gave way. The hand swung about, tearing the branch from Weigall's grasp. The body had been liberated and flung outward, though still submerged by the foam and spray.

Weigall scrambled to his feet and sprang along the rocks, knowing that the danger from suction was over and that Gifford must be carried straight to the quiet pool. Gifford was a fish in the water and could live under it longer than most men. If he survived this, it would not be the first time that his pluck and science had saved him from drowning. Weigall reached the pool. A man in his evening clothes floated on it, his face turned towards a projecting rock over which his arm had fallen, upholding the body. The hand that had held the branch hung limply over the rock, its white reflection visible in the black water. Weigall plunged into the shallow pool, lifted Gifford in his arms and returned to the bank. He laid the body down and threw off his coat that he might be the freer to practice the methods of resuscitation. He was glad of the moment's respite. The valiant life in the man might have been exhausted in that last struggle. He had not dared to look at his face, to put his ear to the heart. The hesitation lasted but a moment. There was no time to lose.

He turned to his prostrate friend. As he did so, something strange and disagreeable smote his senses. For a half-moment he did not appreciate its nature. Then his teeth cracked together, his feet, his outstretched arms pointed towards the woods. But he sprang to the side of the man and bent down and peered into his face. There was no face.

Vanishing Puzzles

&

Brain Teasers

HOW CAN THIS BE TRUE ?

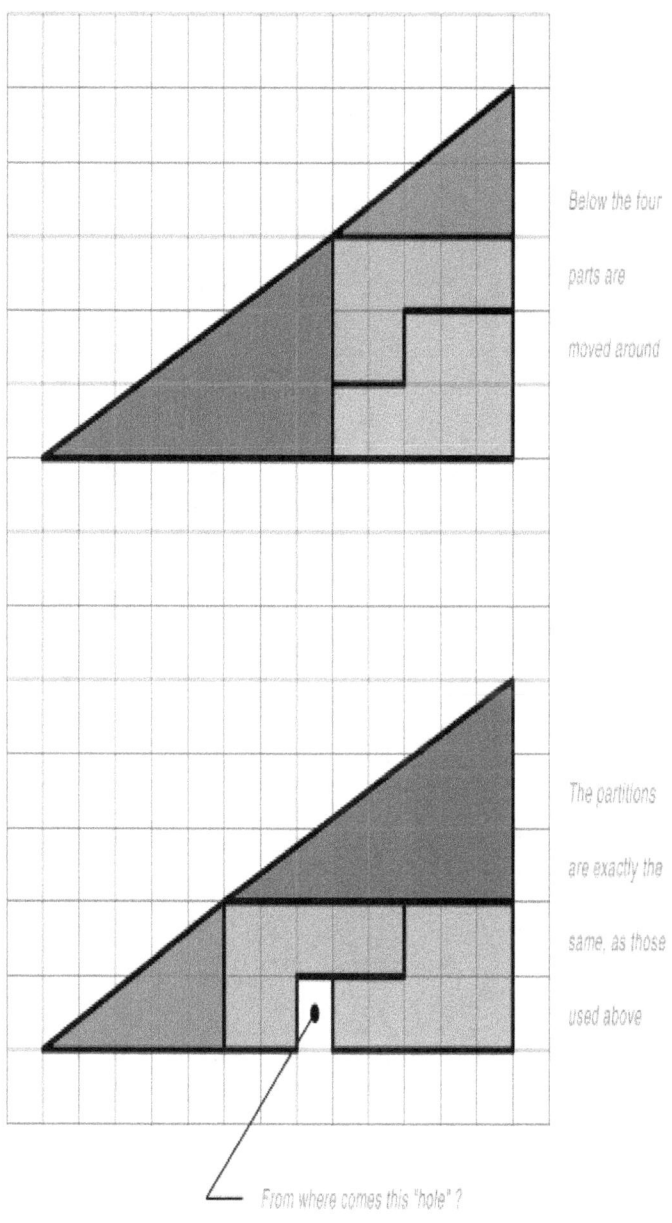

Below the four

parts are

moved around

The partitions

are exactly the

same, as those

used above

From where comes this "hole" ?

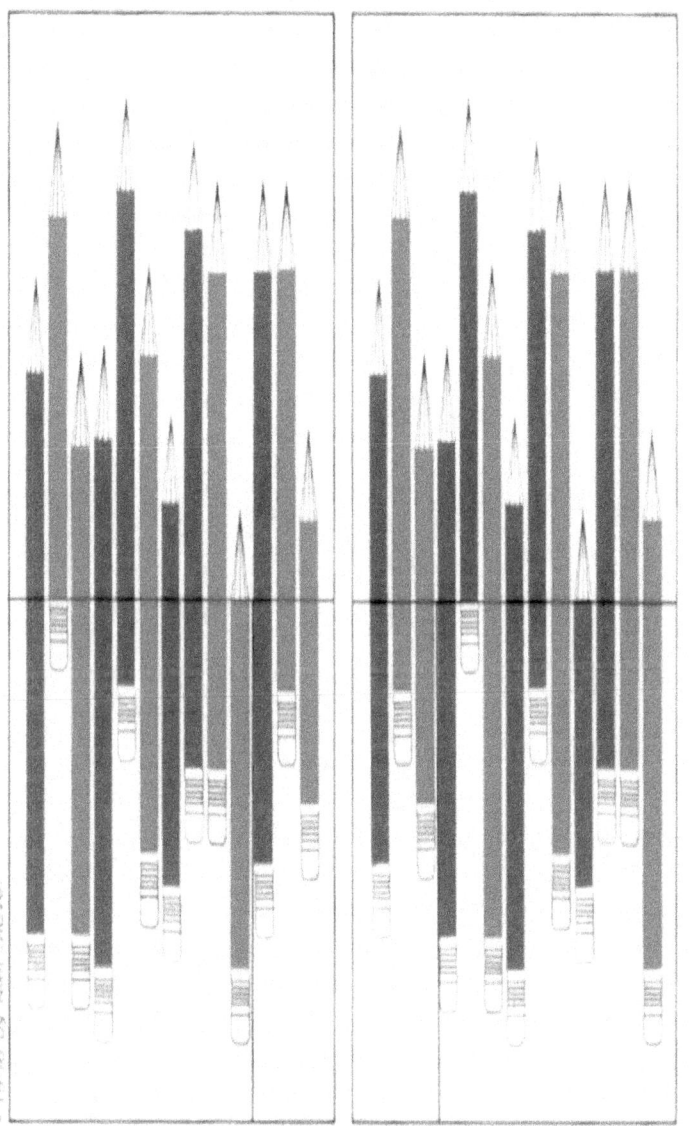

229

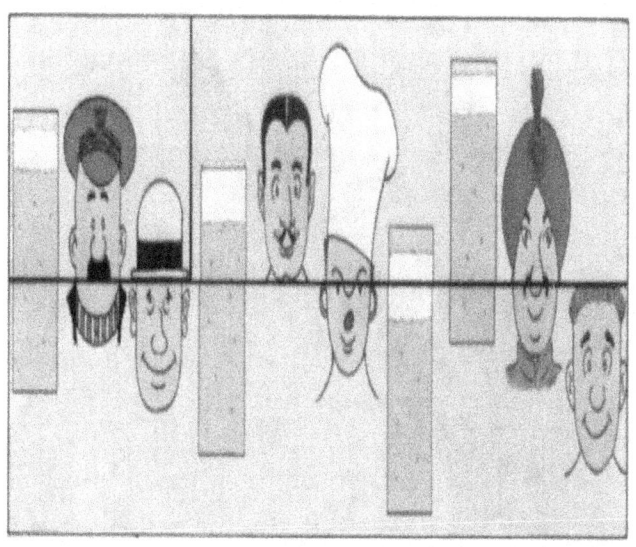

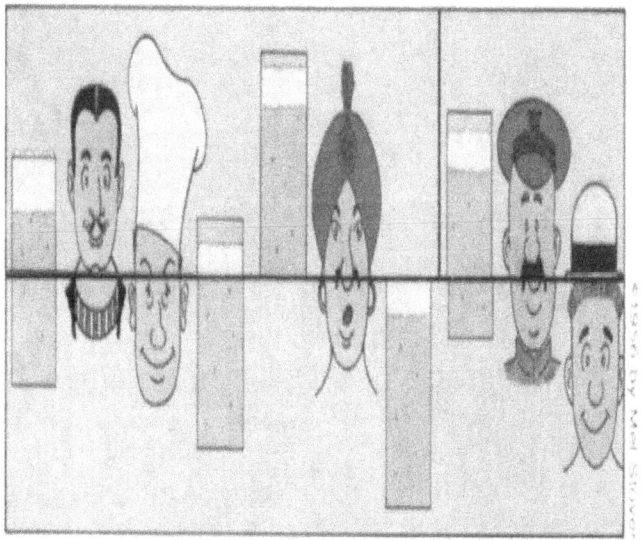

In the author's "Beer Glass Puzzle," 6 men and 4 glasses of beer leave the men two drinks short; but by switching the top two pieces, the situation is corrected, as one new glass appears while one of the men vanishes.

231

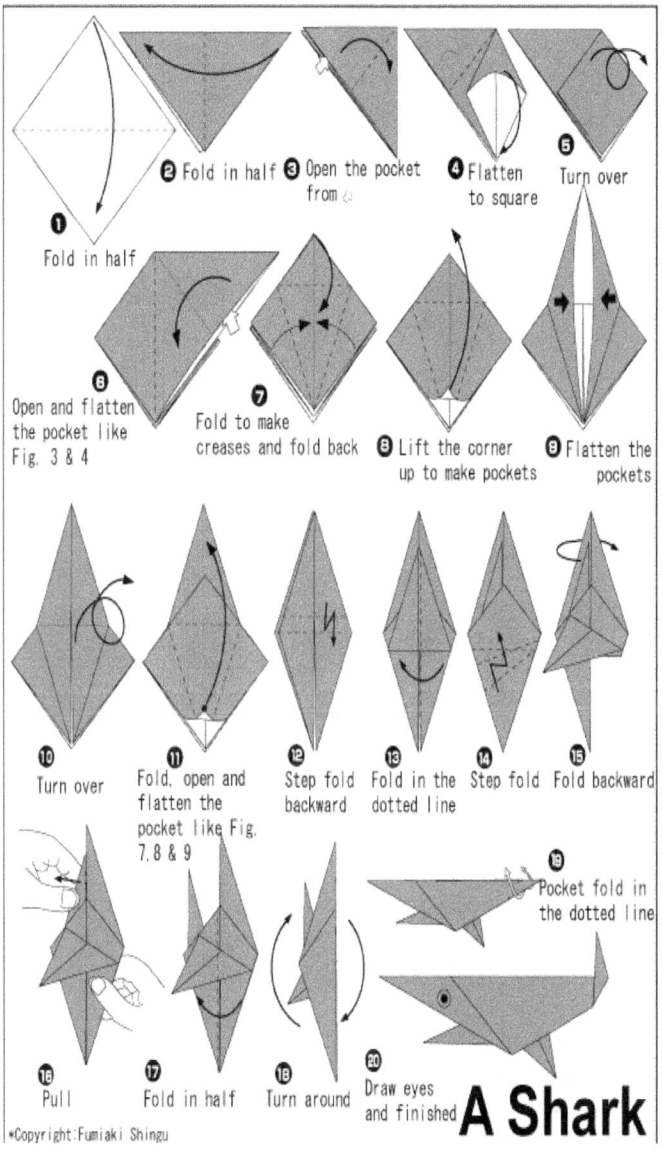

① Fold in half

② Fold in half

③ Open the pocket from

④ Flatten to square

⑤ Turn over

⑥ Open and flatten the pocket like Fig. 3 & 4

⑦ Fold to make creases and fold back

⑧ Lift the corner up to make pockets

⑨ Flatten the pockets

⑩ Turn over

⑪ Fold, open and flatten the pocket like Fig. 7, 8 & 9

⑫ Step fold backward

⑬ Fold in the dotted line

⑭ Step fold

⑮ Fold backward

⑯ Pull

⑰ Fold in half

⑱ Turn around

⑲ Pocket fold in the dotted line

⑳ Draw eyes and finished

A Shark

233

CAN YOU TELL ME?

What occurs twice in a week, once in a year but never in a day?

DON'T OVERTHINK THIS!

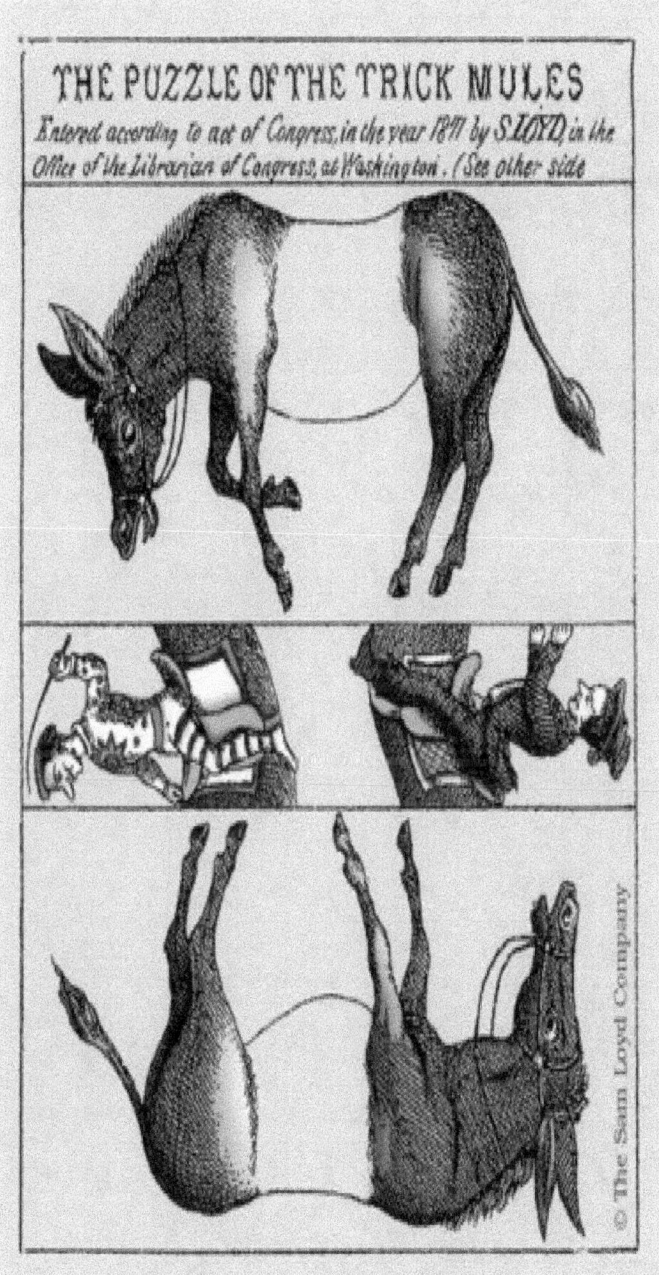

237

Some fairies look just like people. Can you find the fairies on this page? First, draw a line between each description and a person. Then circle the people without a description, they are the fairies!

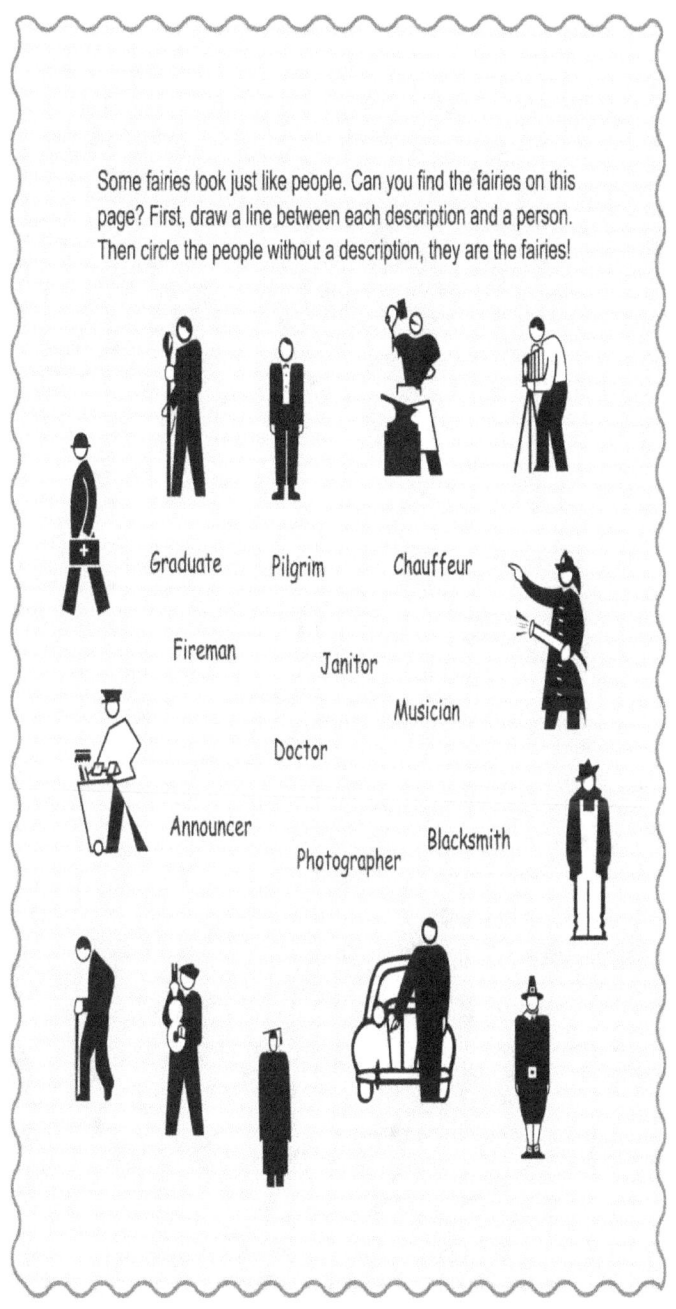

Graduate   Pilgrim   Chauffeur

Fireman   Janitor

Musician

Doctor

Announcer   Blacksmith

Photographer

TIME TRAVEL DEVICES

```
C T W O R M H O L E F O R N P V T F Z R
X I S G W Y C J P G V V Z V Y R L W S L
M P I G U A R D I A N O F F O R E V E R
N L D Y C U K E C Z B X J I H U L O T N
H E R A W L J H Z M Z B M V Q W N I T B
T R A T S N Q E P O I D K E B G M H S Y
O C T C G E B D E L O R E A N E S H E I
O Y E N I H C A M C A B A W T N E S N D
B L E P H O N E B O O T H U O D L P I D
A I K A P P G A W C K G N R H P W L H P
P N J R Z G G J C T F N K N A B C H C O
W D B J J A R S U P E U Q M F L W V A C
R E H S A V Z B N L R R J Y M Y K J M K
Q R R E I F I L P M A N O Y H C A T E E
M B H A A V P E U E T R M Y X V C F M T
D L L I M D A E R T C I M S O C M H I W
V A T A J H A J K V E U E X Z E Z A T A
E R I A D T H E B O X Z O C R O C U Z T
Q O R R R O V O F O M U E R Q I K R J C
X E S O Y A G V V F H O T T U B H Q N H
```

BOOTH
TACHYON AMPLIFIER
COSMIC TREADMILL
TARDIS
DELOREAN
THE BOX
GUARDIAN OF FOREVER
TIME MACHINE
HOT TUB
TIME TUNNEL
MAP
TIPLER CYLINDER
PHONE BOOTH
WABAC MACHINE
POCKET WATCH
WORMHOLE

Can you find them all in time? It's a wibbly-wobbly puzzle, with words moving backwards, forwards, diagonally... and they're all in there. Promise!

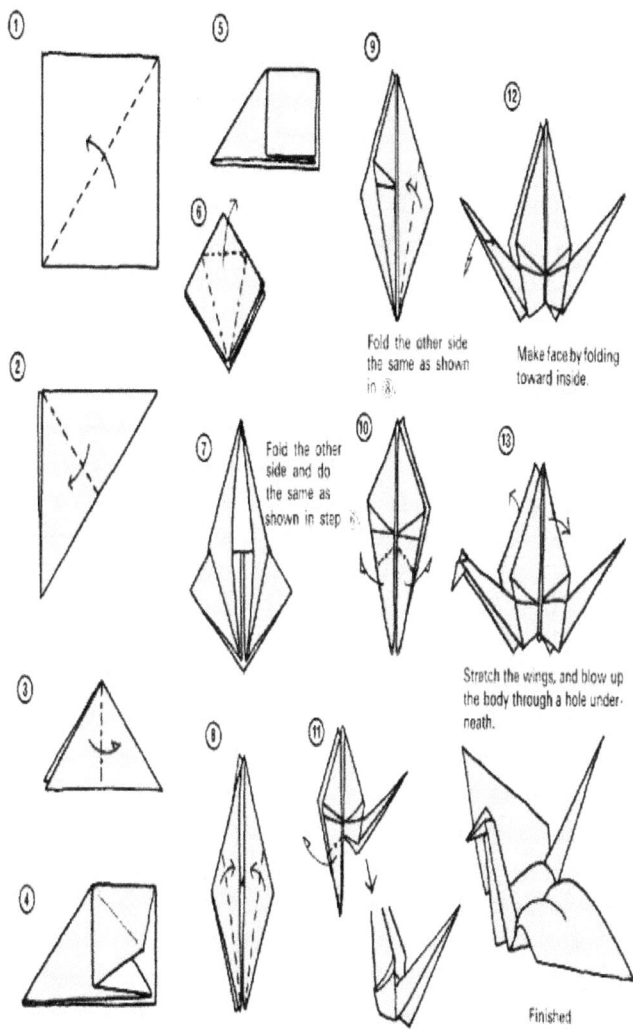

① ⑤ ⑨

⑫

Fold the other side
the same as shown
in 8.

Make face by folding
toward inside.

② ⑥ ⑩

Fold the other
side and do
the same as
shown in step 8.

⑦ ⑬

Stretch the wings, and blow up
the body through a hole underneath.

③ ⑧ ⑪

④

Finished

243

Place 6 X's/No 3 aligned

Healthy *Fast* Food

Sometimes eating on the *fly* is a fact of life. If your busy schedule calls for the occasional grab-and-go meal, Lyn's here to help.

Her research "cheat sheet" identifies two safe bets for lunch or dinner at 10 of the most popular eating chains.

With these menu picks, which each have 480 calories or fewer and are low in artery-clogging saturated fat, you can eat burgers, tacos, and fries guilt-free.

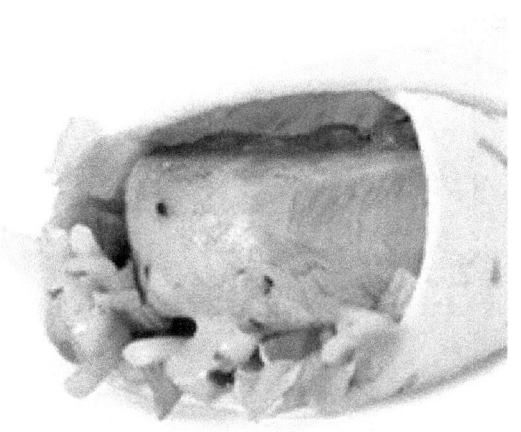

McDonald's

- Premium Caesar Salad with Grilled Chicken and low-fat balsamic vinaigrette plus Fruit 'n Yogurt Parfait; 375 calories, 9.5g fat (4g saturated)
- Grilled Honey Mustard Snack Wrap plus small french fries; 480 calories, 19g fat (5g saturated

Taco Bell

- Fresco Steak Burrito Supreme plus black beans; 430 calories, 10.5g fat (3g saturated)
- Fresco Chicken Soft Taco plus Pintos 'n' Cheese; 330 calories, 10.5g fat (4g saturated)

Dunkin' Donuts

- Egg White Veggie Wake-Up Wrap plus hash browns; 350 calories, 18g fat (4.5g saturated)
- Tuna Salad Sandwich on an English muffin; 390 calories, 23g fat (3.5g saturated)

Subway

- 6" Subway Club on 9-Grain Wheat Bread with lettuce, tomatoes, onions, green peppers, cucumbers, and Sweet Onion Sauce plus apple slices; 445 calories, 4.5g fat (1.5g saturated)
- Oven Roasted Chicken Salad with tomatoes, green peppers, onions, olives, and cucumbers with honey-mustard dressing plus Yogurt Parfait; 400 calories, 6g fat (1.5g saturated)

Starbucks

- Chicken & Hummus Bistro Box (hummus, grilled chicken, grape tomatoes, cucumber, and pita bread) plus a banana; 380 calories, 7g fat (1.2g saturated)
- Zesty Chicken & Black Bean Salad Bowl (grilled chicken, black beans, roasted corn, jicama, tomatoes, feta, greens, and quinoa with chili vinaigrette) plus Seasonal Harvest Fruit Blend; 450 calories, 15g fat (2.5g saturated)

Chipotle

- 3 Barbacoa (braised beef) Tacos on soft corn tortillas with lettuce and tomato salsa; 405 calories, 10g fat (2.5g saturated)
- Vegetarian Burrito Bowl with brown rice, black beans, fajita vegetables, lettuce, and roasted chili-corn salsa; 385 calories, 7g fat (1g saturated)

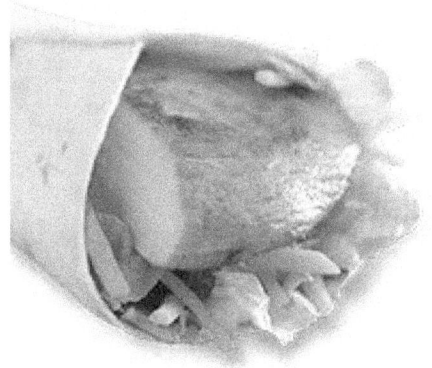

Wendy's

- Large Chili plus Garden Side Salad (no croutons) with fat-free French dressing 375 calories, 9 g fat (3.5 g saturated)
- Ultimate Chicken Grill Sandwich plus apple slices 440 calories, 10 g fat (1.5 g saturated)

Panera

- Half Smoked Turkey Breast on Artisan Whole Grain Loaf plus Low-Fat Garden Vegetable with Pesto Soup (from the You Pick Two Menu); 320 calories, 6g fat (1g saturated)
- Power Mediterranean Chicken Salad (no bacon) plus Baked Lays Potato Chips; 430 calories, 17g fat (2.5g saturated)

Burger King

- Whopper Jr. (no mayo) plus Value-Sized Onion Rings; 410 calories, 18g fat (5.5g saturated)
- Veggie Burger plus apple slices; 440 calories, 16g fat (2.5g saturated)

KFC

- 4 Hot Wings plus Sweet Kernel Corn; 380 calories, 16.5g fat (4g saturated)
- Kentucky Grilled Chicken Breast plus mashed potatoes (without gravy) 310 calories; 10g fat (2.5g saturated)

+ 10

More Calorie Bargains

Whether you're craving a sweet snack or looking for lunch, here are more surprisingly diet-friendly finds.

▼

- Burger King 4-piece Chicken Nuggets; 190 calories, 11g fat (2g saturated)
- Chipotle Cheese Quesadilla (kids' size); 190 calories, 11g fat (6g saturated)
- Dunkin' Donuts Cinnamon Cake Munchkins (two) ; 120 calories, 7g fat (3g saturated)
- KFC Original Recipe Chicken Drumstick; 120 calories, 7g fat (1.5g saturated)
- McDonald's Vanilla Soft-Serve Cone; 170 calories, 4.5g fat (3g saturated)
- Panera Power Breakfast Egg White Bowl with Roasted Turkey; 190 calories, 7g fat (1g saturated)
- Starbucks Chocolate Cake Pop; 140 calories, 7g fat (4g saturated)
- Subway Kids' Roast Beef Sandwich; 200 calories, 3g fat (1g saturated)
- Taco Bell Cool Ranch Doritos Locos Taco; 160 calories, 10g fat (3.5g saturated)
- Wendy's Jr. Original Chocolate Frosty; 200 calories, 5g fat (3.5g saturated)

On The Go Foods –
Made by You

Yogurt Popsicles

Ingredients

Yogurt (non-fat vanilla OR get creative!)

Fruit: thin sliced (I used kiwi, strawberries, and blueberries)

Directions

Add a little yogurt to mold, slide fruit slices down the sides if you want them to show and look pretty. Add more yogurt and them more fruit until mold is full.

Note: You can also chop your fruit small and combine it with the yogurt- then pour into molds and freeze. (Work better with the small, narrow molds.)

Unmold and serve with granola if desired.

Sun Butter Berry Wrap

INGREDIENTS

- 1 whole grain tortilla
- 2 tablespoons of peanut butter or almond butter OR **Sun Butter made from Sunflower Seeds**
- 1 small banana, sliced
- 1 handful of berries (blueberries, raspberries, etc.)
- sliced almonds or crushed walnuts to sprinkle on top
- ground cinnamon (optional)

- agave syrup (optional)

Directions

Lightly spread about 2 tablespoons of peanut butter on the tortilla and top with banana slices, berries, nuts and cinnamon. Lightly drizzle some agave syrup over all the ingredients if you want more sweetness.

Roll up into a wrap or burrito. Enjoy with a glass of cold almond milk.

Easy Egg Frittata

Here's just 1 example of how you can throw together a simple frittata.

Ingredients:

- 1 tablespoon coconut oil or fat of choice
- 1 cup emergency protein (whatever cooked meat you have on hand)
- 1 cup frozen broccoli (or any leftover or frozen veggies)
- 4 large pastured eggs
- 2 tablespoons coconut milk
- 1 teaspoon kosher salt
- Freshly-ground black pepper

First, preheat the toaster oven to 350°F and heat the coconut oil in an 8-inch cast iron skillet over medium heat. Then, add whatever protein you have on hand (here, I used some leftover spicy lamb merguez sausage and onions) to the skillet and stir-fry until heated through.

Meanwhile, place the frozen broccoli in a medium microwave-safe bowl, cover it with a wet paper towel and nuke it until it's thawed. Use a pair of kitchen shears or a knife to cut the broccoli into bite-sized pieces.

Add the broccoli to the ingredients in the pan and mix to cook thoroughly.

Crack the eggs into a medium bowl, and add the coconut milk, salt, and a few grinds of pepper.

Pour the egg mixture into the skillet and cook for 3 to 5 minutes or until the bottom of the frittata is set.

Place the skillet in the oven. Cook for 10 to 15 minutes, and then crank the heat up to broil for another 2 minutes or until the frittata puffs up and is cooked all the way through.

Carefully transfer the frittata to a plate, slice, and serve.

The frittata is delicious cold so it's perfect.

Super Toast

Ingredients

- 2 slices sandwich bread (see note above)
- 1 cup homemade or store-bought vegan refried beans
- 1 avocado, thinly sliced
- A few slivers white onion
- Coarse sea salt such as Maldon or fleur de sel.

Procedure

Toast bread to desired level of doneness. Top with refried beans and avocado (mash with a fork if desired). Add slivered onions, sprinkle with salt, and serve.

Legal Stuff

About the Author

Lyn Murray writes for you, the reader.

She is fascinated by anything that has to do with the supernatural, the paranormal. It's led her to become the author **Who Goes There: The Legend of Tally Bottom Ridge, and Blooded [Anunnaki Rising]** but she doesn't want you to confuse Blooded for just some young adult supernatural thriller with love triangles, vampires, werewolves, zombies, or dystopian societies. Blooded [Anunnaki Rising] blends the supernatural with what is perceived as mythological, historical fiction, [in which there may be more truth than fiction] while leaving readers considering the possibility that her spin on vampires might just be the real truth behind the legend.

A prolific writer of fiction, Lyn has more than a dozen books available for Kindle lovers, including two children's books in the "Little Book of Memories" series, which are also available in hard copy, and creative novella's that capture Lyn's diverse writing style, that include horror stories, stories filled with mystery and intrigue, ghost stories, love stories, and more.

An intuitive, hopeless romantic, Lyn loves science fiction, horror, and spirituality (but don't confuse that for being supportive of mainstream religion). Her family has a politically rich history and is tied to the American Revolution. When she's not playing World of Warcraft with her son, researching natural healing methods, or feeding the ducks in her lake, she's spinning tales of mysterious what-ifs for you.

A virtual recluse in her home, *Villa Le Paradis Sur Terre*, Lyn spends her days researching, reading, writing, and enjoying the simple things in life with her husband, such as a good cup of coffee and quiet conversation. The back of her Villa is glass from floor to ceiling and overlooks a private lake. I would say, that if ever there was truth in a statement, Lyn is living proof that people who live in glass houses shouldn't throw stones . . . they should be writers.

Go to YouTube [copy and past the link below] for Lyn Murray's Book Trailers:
http://www.youtube.com/channel/UCxds7uuT4IMB RPLiYTNCGBQ?feature=watch

◇◇◇

Credits

This has been a
Golden Panda Publishing production.

. . . Golden Panda Publishing on Google . . .

https://sites.google.com/site/goldenpandapublishing/home

You'll find Lyn Murray there.

◇◇◇

You'll also find Lyn Murray on Amazon.com:

http://www.amazon.com/Lyn-
Murray/e/B00ANT6E3A/ref=sr_tc_2_0?qid=1379005721&sr=1-2-ent

&

Lyn's Website:

Just GOOGLE . . . Lyn Murray Writes

Or

Lyn Murray Writes 2

http://lynmurray.wix.com/lynmurray

◇◇◇

A special thanks goes out to all those nameless souls
who provided such wonderful research material via
Public Domain sources around the WWW.

◇◇◇

Other Books by Lyn

Little Book of Memories, Vol. 1
Little Book of Memories, Vol. 2
One Dark Halloween Night
The Howling Man
The Tuck
Nightfall's Day
Glasses Glasses
Paula [A Nightmare]
The 3rd Sunday of Every Month
[Mystery of White Rose Cemetery]
Who Goes There?
[The Legend of Tally Bottom Ridge]
A Case of Jitters
[Murder at Hammond Hill Rectory]
B.E.K. [Black Eyed Kid's Phenomenon]

▼ ▼ ▼ and of course ▼ ▼ ▼

BLOODED [Anunnaki Rising]
BLOODED – NOMADS [Anunnaki Tribulation]
BLOODED – CINDER [Anunnaki Armageddon]

♦♦♦ with more on the way ♦♦♦

▼ ▼ ▼ Watch for ▼ ▼ ▼
The Wilde Side
Peter Wilde Detective
Coming Soon!

◇◇◇

◇◇◇

. . . Golden Panda Publishing on Google . . .

HTTPS://SITES.GOOGLE.COM/SITE/GOLDENPANDAPUBLISHING/HOME

YOU'LL FIND LYN MURRAY THERE.

◇◇◇

Lyn's website:

Just GOOGLE . . . Lyn Murray Writes

https://sites.google.com/site/lynmurraywrites/home

OR

Lyn Murray Writes 2

http://lynmurray.wix.com/lynmurray

◇◇◇

Thank You!

I'm honored that you took the time to read my book, and really hope you liked it! If you could, take a moment to let me know what you liked about it, I'd really like to know. Your feedback helps me hone my skills. I'm always looking for new ideas, and developing characters and story plots.

Tell me what kind of stories you like –
I write for you!

See ya soon. Bye!

www.ingramcontent.com/pod-product-compliance
Lightning Source LLC
Chambersburg PA
CBHW070630290526
45790CB00001B/64